Demons Release Trilogies

THE PREQUEL
Book 3

Mission: To Proclaim Transformation and Truth
Publisher: Transformed Publishing
Email: transformedpublishing@gmail.com
Website: www.transformedpublishing.com

Copyright © 2021 by Liberty Crouch

All rights reserved solely by the author. No part of this book may be reproduced, stored in a retrieval system, or transmitted in any form or by any means without expressed written permission of the author.

All content was provided to the publisher as original author work, not infringing on the copyrights of others.

Scripture is taken from the New King James Version ®, unless otherwise noted. Copyright © 1982 by Thomas Nelson. Used by permission. All rights reserved.

Amplified Bible (AMP) Copyright © 2015 by The Lockman Foundation, La Habra, CA 90631. All rights reserved.

Holman Christian Standard Bible (HCSB) Copyright © 1999, 2000, 2002, 2003, 2009 by Holman Bible Publishers, Nashville Tennessee. All rights reserved.

King James Version (KJV) Public Domain

The Message (MSG) Copyright © 1993, 2002, 2018 by Eugene H. Peterson

New International Version (NIV) Holy Bible, New International Version®, NIV® Copyright ©1973, 1978, 1984, 2011 by Biblica, Inc.® Used by permission. All rights reserved worldwide.

New Living Translation (NLT) *Holy Bible*, New Living Translation, copyright © 1996, 2004, 2015 by Tyndale House Foundation. Used by permission of Tyndale House Publishers, Inc., Carol Stream, Illinois 60188. All rights reserved.

Living Bible (TLB) The Living Bible copyright © 1971 by Tyndale House Foundation. Used by permission of Tyndale House Publishers Inc., Carol Stream, Illinois 60188. All rights reserved.

The Passion Translation (TPT) The Passion Translation®. Copyright © 2017, 2018, 2020 by Passion & Fire Ministries, Inc. Used by permission. All rights reserved. thePassionTranslation.com

The Voice (VOICE) The Voice Bible Copyright © 2012 Thomas Nelson, Inc. The Voice™ translation © 2012 Ecclesia Bible Society All rights reserved.

ISBN: 978-1-953241-21-4
Printed in the U.S.A.

Demons Release Trilogies

THE PREQUEL
Book 3

Liberty Crouch

Acknowledgements

To the overcomers,

Grace and peace to all who read and glory to the Lord for all who hear and are impacted by the writings within these pages.

… "Now salvation and power are set in place,
 and the kingdom reign of our God
 and the ruling authority of his Anointed One
 are established.
For the accuser of our brothers and sisters,
 who relentlessly accused them
 day and night before our God,
 has now been defeated—cast out once and for all!
They conquered him completely
 through the blood of the Lamb
 and the powerful word of his testimony.
They triumphed because they did not love and cling
 to their own lives, even when faced with death.
  Revelation 12:10-11 (TPT)

Preface

Welcome. You have in your hand *Book 3,* of the *Demons Release Trilogies.* Keep in mind *Book 1* is the author's before Christ story and is spoken from the perspective of a lost soul. *Book 2* articulately displays the author's transformation and shares her miraculous testimonies in Christ. The fullness of the gospel and the way to salvation is expressed through the perspective of a renewed mind. *Book 3* goes back in time. It shares the author's very first journal writings, which were compiled while going through withdrawals during her first months of recovery.

Book 3 Part 1 shares the backstory. Part 2 is filled with true doctor reports and *Any Thoughts* journaling sections for the reader to interact with the text to better reveal and analyze their own thoughts. This will help you learn how some people in the medical field operate and understand that doctors are people too. They do not know everything, nor do they have the final say. The author is a living testimony to the truth that God has the final say. *Book 3* Part 3 is filled with engaging testimonies; letters of hope from each one of her children who have been reconciled back to her; and a letter from God's Throne Room to you, the reader, empathizing your *God-given Identity, Purpose*, and *Authority*. The closing section of this book shares Scriptures of hope - full of promises for your soul to prosper. The armor of God is explained to equip you for today and upcoming days.

Demons Release Trilogies is a tool and can be used as a workbook personally or in group settings for ministry, recovery, revival, and deliverance. It is a weapon against darkness for the Glory of God. You cannot judge a book by its cover. *Demons Release Trilogies* is no threat to any territory by the cover page. When you begin to read and dig into it, you will discover the heart and soul of Jesus Christ. He came to seek and save the lost, deliver us from the evil one, heal our souls, bring us out of captivity, rescue us, comfort us, help us, resurrect us, and bring us back into right standing with the Father.

"I am thankful we are journeying together.

Let my transparency be for your revival!"

—Liberty Crouch

Table of Contents

To the Readers of My Dreams 1
Introduction 3

Part I – Inner Child

Phone Art: What Do *You* See? Inner Child 5
C.I.T. – Inner Child 6
C.I.T. – Journal to Doc 8
C.I.T. – The Program 10
C.I.T. – Question Doc 12
C.I.T. – Liberty's Rules 15
C.I.T. – Daily Grind 17
C.I.T. – Doc 19
C.I.T. – Report 21
C.I.T. – Who What When How Why 23
C.I.T. – Hey Doc – Analyze This 25
C.I.T. – Insight Doc 27
C.I.T. – Diagnosis 29
C.I.T. – Analyze This Doc 31
C.I.T. – Memory Game 33
C.I.T. – Who's In Control 34
C.I.T. – A Prayer for Papa 38
C.I.T. – Patience 40
C.I.T. – The Language of the Mayans 42
C.I.T. – Sambrina the Spirit Dog 44
C.I.T. – Get Smoked 45
C.I.T. – Messages 46
C.I.T. – I am an Artist of a New Breed 47
C.I.T. – Similes, Metaphors, Haiku 49
C.I.T. – The Perfect Man 50
C.I.T. – Hide and Seek 52
C.I.T. – Many Men 54
C.I.T. – More to Frank Than Meets the Eye 56
C.I.T. – Pharmaceutical Schemes 58
C.I.T. – Veins 59
C.I.T. – Para What 61
C.I.T. – The Urge 62
C.I.T. – Characteristics & Traits 64
C.I.T. – Mission 67

Part II – The Mission

Phone Art: What Do *You* See?
    Save a Life, Live a Life 69
Part II – The Mission 70

Table of Contents

Part II – Intro to The Mission _____ 72
Intro to Generational Cycles:
    The Letter from My Mom _____ 75
Testimony from My Mom: Victim No More _____ 77
Mom's Doctor Report – 1 _____ 81
Mom's Doctor Report – 2 _____ 82
Mom's Doctor Report – 3 _____ 83
Mom's Doctor Report – 4 _____ 84
Poem – Life (written by my daughter) _____ 86
Poem – In America (written by my daughter) _____ 88
Journal Entry: Counseling Session Prior to the
    Release of My Personal Medical Records _____ 91
Medical Records _____ 92
Entry 1 – Client Access Record Permission _____ 95
Entry 2 – Note Date: 07/23/2010 _____ 96
Entry 3 – Note Date: 08/09/2010 Diagnosis _____ 97
Entry 4 – Reasons for Seeking Services _____ 98
Entry 5 – Reasons for Seeking Services _____ 99
Entry 6 – Substance Abuse Dependence History &
    Relevant Family History _____ 101
Entry 7 – Current Mental Status _____ 102
Entry 8 – Assessment Interpretation _____ 103
Entry 9 – Goals Confessed _____ 104
Entry 10 – Action Plan _____ 104
Entry 11 – Dr. Sandy Encounter Date: 08/09/2010 ___ 106
Entry 12 – Note Date: 09/13/2010 _____ 106
Entry 13 – Note Date: 09/21/2010 _____ 107
Entry 14 – Continued Note _____ 108
Entry 15 – Note Date: 01/03/2011 _____ 109
Entry 16 – Note Date: 04/25/2011 _____ 110
Entry 17 – Note Date: 06/02/2011 _____ 111
Entry 18 – Note Date: 10/04/2011 _____ 112
Entry 19 – Note Date: 11/10/2011 _____ 113
Entry 20 – Medication Management
    Date: 02/06/2012 _____ 114
Entry 21 – Note Date: 02/06/2012
    No Medications Found _____ 115
Entry 22 – Continued Note _____ 116
Entry 23 – Note Date: 05/21/2012 _____ 117
Entry 24 – Continued Note _____ 118
Entry 25 – Note Date: 08/17/2012 _____ 119
Entry 26 – Continued Note _____ 120
Entry 27 – Continued Note _____ 121

Table of Contents

Entry 28 – Note Date: 12/31/2012
    Medication Management & Evaluation_____123
Entry 29 – Continued Note_____124
Entry 30 – Diagnosis as of 12/31/2012_____125
Entry 31 – Note Date 01/23/2013 Problem Depression____126
Entry 32 – Continued Note_____127
Entry 33 – The Battle of the Mind_____129
Entry 34 – Note Date 01/28/2013_____130
Entry 35 – Next Up the Psychologist
    Date: 02/04/2013_____131
Entry 36 – Initial Contact Report from the Psychologist
    Date: 02/04/2013_____132
Entry 37 – Continued Report_____133
Entry 38 – Home Therapist Note Date: 02/14/2013_____135
Entry 39 – Psychiatrist Note Date: 02/14/2013_____136
Entry 40 – Psychologist Note Date: 02/18/2013_____137
Entry 41 – Home Therapist Note Date: 02/20/2013_____138
Entry 42 – Home Therapist Note Date: 02/27/2013 _____139
Entry 43 – Home Therapist Note Date: 03/08/2013_____141
Entry 44 – Home Therapist Note Date: 04/02/2013_____142
Entry 45 – Home Therapist Note Date: 04/08/2013 _____143
Entry 46 – Psychiatrist Note Date: 04/08/2013_____144
Entry 47 – Vitals Check Note Date: 04/08/2013_____145
Entry 48 – Home Therapist Note Date: 04/10/2013_____147
Entry 49 – Home Therapist Note Date: 04/24/2013_____148
Entry 50 – Home Therapist Note Date: 05/03/2013_____149
Entry 51 – Home Therapist Note Date: 05/07/2013_____150
Entry 52 – Home Therapist Note Date: 05/10/2013_____151
Entry 53 – Home Therapist Note Date: 05/15/2013_____153
Entry 54 – Home Therapist Note Date: 05/22/2013_____154
Entry 55 – Home Therapist Note Date: 05/28/2013_____155
Entry 56 – Home Therapist Note Date: 05/31/2013_____156
Entry 57 – Home Therapist Note Date: 06/03/2013_____157
Entry 58 – Home Therapist Note Date: 06/05/2013_____159
Entry 59 – Home Therapist Note Continued_____160
Entry 60 – Home Therapist Note Date: 06/07/2013_____161
Entry 61 – The Vein of Love Surgery_____162
Entry 62 & 63 – The Vein of Love Surgery_____163
False Positive Drug Tests_____167

Part III – The Lamb

Phone Art: What Do *You* See? Blessings and Curses_____169
A Test: I Let the Devil in My House_____171

Table of Contents

They Said I Wouldn't Make It
    A Letter from My Oldest Son_____175
Through Thick and Thin_____176
There is Power in the Name of Jesus_____177
Why I Pray - A Testimony_____181
A Letter to My Past, Present, and Future_____183
The Love Letter from Heaven's Throne Room to You
    Identity, Purpose, and Authority Revealed_____188
Promises of God_____199
Write_____205
What's to Come & Stay Connected_____212

To the Readers of My Dreams

To the readers of my dreams, I gave it to you raw and truthfully and you chose to stay with me.

In the first part of *Book 3*, you will read sporadic thoughts and feelings that I journaled and later formed into C.I.T.s (C.reative I.nspirational T.hinking), throughout my recovery from the lifelong disease of drug addiction and fighting mental illnesses, on and off medications, and at my papa's sanctuary, Owl Mountain, beginning July 4, 2010. This is the prequel of my testimony as an overcomer.

You might come to understand my state of mind a little better as you hear these raw unscripted journal entries. I was going through withdrawals, having a loss of reality, and loss of my senses, but still hanging onto hope and acknowledging God, who I did not even know yet.

You might also recognize, not only bipolarism, but multiple personalities and other traits of mental illnesses that are noted in the entries of the doctor reports included in Part II. Various spiritual theology is intertwined within the words I chose to use at the time of these writings. Some of the named personalities / voices you will hear are *L*; the Doc, P.I., Mammamia, and the Ice Princess, along with parts being narrated by myself, Liberty Crouch, the author and illustrator of the *Demons Release Trilogies*; all in search of my true identity.

As you continue to read Part II, you will see scanned original documents from my past psychiatrists, psychologists, doctors, and finally, *The Vein of Love,* my plastic surgeon's report, which was the result of shooting methamphetamines into my breast. You can look back to the C.I.T. titled, *Vein of Love* in *Book One*, Part I to understand. I have also included noted entries from my home therapist who documented a close walk with me during my recovery.

Part III of this final book of the *Demons Release Trilogies*, is full of hope, testimonies of overcoming, redemption in my life as a mother, and life-giving promises from the One who created us. You will

Liberty Crouch

notice a transformation of my mind taking place. My thoughts have dramatically shifted from Part I of this book.

For my readers with love, may you get what you need from this trilogy, if not for you, for someone you know or love. May it bless you as it has me.

Inspired by God Almighty our Creator. He's been pushing my pen the whole way. *L.*

C.reative I.nspirational T.hinking (C.I.T.)

Demons Release
a unified trilogy
from the epitome of where i speak

a God given gift
for you
from Him and me

a blessing from the sky indeed
my true set path
of destiny

Introduction

Tangible evidence is not faith.
Tangible evidence is the substance of faith.

Book Three
The Prequel to Book One, my before Christ story.

    In this third book of the *Demons Release Trilogies*, a three-part book series; I take you all on the journey to answer the mysterious, *whys*. We go back in time, before *Book One* ever existed and find out how *Book Two* came to be.

    This story takes place before I ever met Jesus Christ and before some of the experiences mentioned in *Book One*. I bring to the readers of my dreams, tangible evidence for the mind of logic and reasoning, to hopefully bring you out from the intellect and into walking by faith; not by sight.

    For the making of this prequel, my mom was so kind to allow me to use her own personal doctor reports. These reports came from completely different doctors than mine, at a completely different place and time than any doctor reports you will see while examining mine. I included this information to demonstrate how they are comparably similar in diagnosis and history.

    Remember, I shared with you in the first two books that my mom didn't raise me nor my siblings, her mother didn't raise her nor her siblings, and I didn't raise my three children. So how is it possible for my mother, my daughter, and myself, to have similar character traits? I also bring to you evidence of similar generational thought patterns shown in the unique testimony written by my mom herself; my daughter's poetry at age 9 (included in *Book One*); along with a recent poem my daughter wrote as a teenager from her perspective, through her own personal life experiences, which seem to be the effect of sinful behaviors passed down to her generationally. Throughout this prequel, I share raw unscripted journal entries of the inner most thoughts that plagued my mind which have been written in free verse poetry pulled from my journals beginning in 2010 – the start of my journey towards my recovery.

    Tangible evidence is presented throughout this book, showing generational curses passed down to children from the sin of a parent. Even through the eyes of logic and beyond a reasonable doubt by the world's perspective; this evidence is justifiable. Tangible evidence is also brought to you from a Biblical perspective.

The purpose of this prequel is to allow the readers of my dreams to have a choice, to choose, and to know there is something Greater to choose from. While reading the pages of this book, you may experience conviction of righteousness from the power of the Holy Spirit, who gives you the grace you will need to change things within yourself. You will have an opportunity, at some point, to decide for yourself if you want to break the generational curses off your own lineage. Knowing this beforehand, I encourage you to take your time reading, comparing, researching, and most of all, having ears to hear what the Holy Spirit is saying to you. Maintain an open heart to receive His revelation and knowledge, which could change the course of not only your eternal destiny, but future generations.

As I open my life to you, the readers of my dreams; once again I thank you for being open to receive the very Truth that may save the lives of this generation and generations to come.

This unique book has been specifically formatted to create interaction between the reader and the writings within this book. You will see sections at the bottom of many of the pages titled: *Enlighten Me* and *Any Thoughts*.

You will hear my present-day voice, now in Christ, throughout the *Enlighten Me* sections. Through discernment, my desire is to help each reader fully understand the key principles being shared. *Read between the lines* is being interpreted.

Each reader has an opportunity to engage with each thought shared and to come to a deeper understanding of the free verse poetry, testimonies, and the doctor reports in the *Any Thoughts* sections. This journal space is to take notes and reflect how the information shared on each page can impact your own life.

At the end of this book, there is a designated area to write out a plan of action based on all the interactive notes you have jotted down throughout the pages.

> *Legacy for me, is to leave footsteps of Faith for you. I have been richly blessed with eyes to see and ears to hear. May your journey of Faith leave behind a legacy of tangible evidence that leads many back home to our Heavenly Father.*
>
> *Butterfly Kisses, L.*

Part I – Inner Child

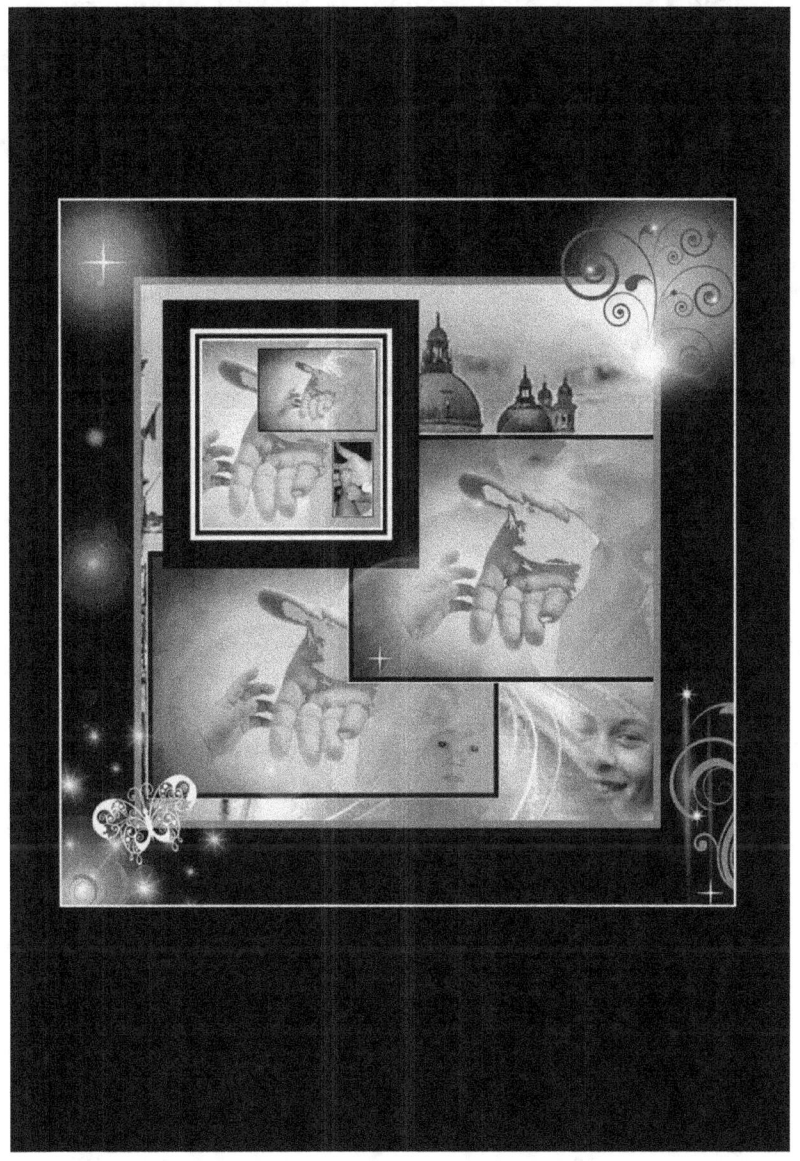

Phone Art: What Do *You* See?
Inner Child

Inner Child: A person's supposed original or true self, especially when regarded as damaged or concealed by negative childhood experiences.

C.I.T. - Inner Child

memories come joggin so fast
recollections of my past

constantly fighting feelings of disgust
disturbance in the turbulence
in my thoughts

turn cold only if you knew
the inner child that cries
died a couple times and came back alive

i get reminded of times
instances and crimes
committed against me

the feelings can't hide
meds block heads block me

from being free

can't you see the inner child
no peace

Enlighten Me

Bad memories of hurtful trauma and wounds from early childhood begin to surface. Memories of when sexual predators had their way with me and my sister. Two separate instances and two totally different predators committed sexual acts upon my little sister and myself, even before I was 5 years old.

Years of suppressed feelings, emotional distress, and unresolved trauma wounds that were never dealt with, truly do take a toll on the mental health of a person. That is exactly why I was self-medicating to escape the reality of the suppressed pain of it all. The more medications the doctors gave me for the symptoms of bipolarism, anxiety, sleeplessness, and high blood pressure, the more it perpetuated the very pain I was trying to express. My desire was true freedom, but I did not quite know how to get it.

One of my familiar self-defense mechanisms was to be really mean to the people around me so that I could hurt them before they would have a chance to hurt me. To turn *cold* means to turn cold hearted. That is a character trait of the personality, *Ice Princess*.

Died a couple of times, is a mix of literal and figurative symbolic expressions toward the memories of suicidal attempts, drug overdoses, people literally trying to kill me, and finally dying to myself so I can truly live.

Any Thoughts

_____
_____
_____
_____
_____
_____
_____
_____

Liberty Crouch

C.I.T. – Journal to Doc

analyze this

i will soon overcome this addictive personality
by conquering all the demons
retraining my brain
by organizing filing thoughts
notes details
C.I.T.s and theories
phone art
memory games
and doin it all at a challenge

i will overcome and adapt
any situation and enter my realm
of completion

thanks to my Spirit guides
for bringing a process to my brain and retraining

mammamia signing out

Enlighten Me

I can hear thoughts of determination and a sense of hope. This specific journal entry was written from the personality, *Mammamia*, who we will get to know more about as we continue to read.

For bringing a process to my brain and retraining, sounds like what I'm doing now – consistent repetition through the making of these books. For example: Writing in my journals, following the steps to publishing, editing each, and creating images from my cell phone to become illustrations for this book as a whole.

Any Thoughts

_____
_____
_____
_____
_____
_____
_____
_____
_____
_____
_____
_____
_____
_____
_____
_____
_____
_____
_____
_____

Liberty Crouch

C.I.T. – The Program

tryin to mastermind my mind
i come in disguise
and take over all kinds

now i'm burning DVDs and disks
for this and lots of that
phone art viewing in progress

steady smokin
smokin my brain
stayin tame

not scared to conquer and adapt
getting gain sanity

no obesity yet though
next is the regimen and diet
spiritual guidance
zen has diminished
so i create
while i dissipate
growin in ways that i know i'm changin

no more faces
no more anticipation
only making

me wake up to my dreams

peace and quiet day walker
this is note for the dr.

as i analyze my mind
it grows inside

challenges changes and chance
get with the program or make one for yourself

Demons Release Trilogies, Book 3

Enlighten Me

At the time of this writing, I so desired structure. *The Program*, is referring to coming to the realization that I could create healthy daily routines. *Phone art viewing in progress*, was the result of Inspired Images I created from a cell phone application. I learned how to transfer the images to my desktop computer, create a slideshow effect, and then transfer the slideshow to a DVD - *tangible proof* that I was able to do what I put my mind to doing.

Steady smokin, is referring to the first steps in my recovery, when I stopped doing all hard drugs and smoked marijuana and K-2 (synthetic marijuana). Smoking this stuff with an addictive personality created a false sense of courage which resulted in panic attacks and added mental instability. Yet somehow, I was allowed this period of time to detox completely from hard drugs (meth, crack, and cocaine) to get just enough peace to write in my journal and receive the Inspired Creativity that became footsteps forward to where I am today.

How many voices do you hear in the journal entry conversation, *The Program?*

Any Thoughts

_____
_____
_____
_____
_____
_____
_____
_____
_____
_____
_____
_____
_____

Liberty Crouch

C.I.T. – Question Doc

where am i
who do you see
just me or are there at least three
so, we made a list
it will consist of me
and how many i can see

comicidilac-kinda funny
liberty
lib
L.-one of a kind wild in the mind
ice princess-hot flashes and cold in an instant
mammamia writer inspires

personalities take note
who's the big shot

ice princess-is hot on the outside but turns cold at the blink of an eye
P.rivate **I**.nvestigator-smokes tokes talks it out to myself investigates
takes notes and speaks aloud
tourette syndrome
mammamia-puts on her readers and writes to the dreamer's ear
comicidilac-well she's the funny one lots a fun
L.-is who i've become on this journey that is lately
she takes the cake special creative
Liberty-that's me too the wild side free spirit kinda careless at times

but question doc
who am i

could it be
i'm my own **P.I.**
Lib why?

Demons Release Trilogies, Book 3

Enlighten Me

So many personalities with different voices. I hear the enemy's voice of confusion bringing disorder and chaos to my thoughts, by stirring up fear and paranoia.

> For God is not *the author* of confusion but of peace, as in all the churches of the saints.
>
> 1 Corinthians 14:33

So, how then, does a person who has never known the Voice of God Almighty discern between truth and deception – good and evil? In the Holy Bible through the written inspired Scriptures of God, I found the answer. See for yourself:

> And other sheep I have which are not of this fold; them also I must bring, and they will hear My voice; and there will be one flock *and* one shepherd.

> ["]My sheep hear My voice, and I know them, and they follow Me. And I give them eternal life, and they shall never perish; neither shall anyone snatch them out of My hand. My Father, who has given *them* to Me, is greater than all; and no one is able to snatch *them* out of My Father's hand. I and *My* Father are one."
>
> John 10:16; 27-30

> …[A]t that time you were without Christ, being aliens from the commonwealth of Israel and strangers from the covenants of promise, having no hope and without God in the world.

> For He Himself is our peace, who has made both one, and has broken down the middle wall of separation,
>
> Ephesians 2:12, 14

> Paul, an apostle of Jesus Christ by the will of God,
> To the saints who are in Ephesus, and faithful in Christ Jesus:

> Grace to you and peace from God our Father and the Lord Jesus Christ.

> Blessed *be* the God and Father of our Lord Jesus Christ, who has blessed us with every spiritual blessing in the heavenly *places* in

Christ, just as He chose us in Him before the foundation of the world, that we should be holy and without blame before Him in love, having predestined us to adoption as sons by Jesus Christ to Himself, according to the good pleasure of His will, to the praise of the glory of His grace, by which He made us accepted in the Beloved.

In Him we have redemption through His blood, the forgiveness of sins, according to the riches of His grace which He made to abound toward us in all wisdom and prudence, having made known to us the mystery of His will, according to His good pleasure which He purposed in Himself, that in the dispensation of the fullness of the times He might gather together in one all things in Christ, both which are in heaven and which are on earth—in Him. In Him also we have obtained an inheritance, being predestined according to the purpose of Him who works all things according to the counsel of His will, that we who first trusted in Christ should be to the praise of His glory.

Ephesians 1:1-12

Any Thoughts

_____
_____
_____
_____
_____
_____
_____
_____
_____
_____
_____
_____
_____
_____
_____
_____
_____

C.I.T. - Liberty's Rules

laws made up by
someone inside me
no hidin it

always sign align
and make room for improvement
check again did you date and sign it

create your space
your environment

zen music positive support
i write about it
incense space
set goals and make dreams come alive

everything has a home
alignment
no more tourette's outbursts in public
be a lady

so, she signs it
L-the dr.

Enlighten Me

Liberty's Rules are the beginning of establishing a sense of normalcy and order the best way I knew how at that time. I figured out how to arrange my workspace to a functioning, inspirational, place of peace, which at that time was a dusty upstairs loft area partly my bedroom and partly my dad's (papa) living area of his home.

The definition of *zen* is slang for feeling peaceful and relaxed. Not understanding who I was or who I would become yet but knowing there is something inside of me just waiting to be awakened, *The Dr.* became another personality figure. Through *The Dr.*, I identified someone inside of me that knew how to lead well and manage problems and stress levels.

What are some of the areas in your life that need stress management and how do you handle stress? Do you have a vice? What is your go-to?

Any Thoughts

_____
_____
_____
_____
_____
_____
_____
_____
_____
_____
_____
_____
_____
_____
_____
_____
_____
_____

C.I.T. – Daily Grind

regimen and diet
smoke and toke and analyze
mesmerized by the sight

off to work set up office
read book that i wrote

pc in places
keys and notes

ok music zen ready then

put on your face with no makeup
to the office doc after waking up

an accomplishment every day is the way
completion is the way to be pleased

smile laugh often inside and by yourself
i do congratulate and give thanks out loud and in your face

eat when hungry not before
and don't get obsessive over the feast

a snack at night don't turn parasite
h2o is the way to go

got my own spring in the back yard

go with the flow
align sign and follow your own rules
even if you don't wanna listen

step back gain patience
happiness again in view
bliss organization

everything will fall in place

daily grind
work and be happy
love and be loved

always give thanks to the Man above

Liberty Crouch

Enlighten Me

Self-motivation, willpower, disciplining myself to achieve goals each day, all baby steps. God was with me, yes, even while I was still a sinner. Learning to use self-control is learning how to lean into something greater than yourself. Self-control is a fruit of the Holy Spirit.

My desires were starting to come into alignment with the desires of the Lord even though I did not know Him yet. Living on that mountain with my dad, we had unlimited access to running streams of water.

> "So don't worry about these things, saying, 'What will we eat? What will we drink? What will we wear?' These things dominate the thoughts of unbelievers, but your heavenly Father already knows all your needs. Seek the Kingdom of God above all else, and live righteously, and he will give you everything you need.["]
>
> Matthew 6:31-33 (NLT)

Any Thoughts

_____
_____
_____
_____
_____
_____
_____
_____
_____
_____
_____
_____
_____
_____
_____
_____
_____
_____

C.I.T. – Doc

my legs and feet they shake more
when i smoke but i have energy that i don't normally have too
as i lay on my couch and think to myself being my own doc
and talkin it out
words come to my mind

bingeing and persona
binge bingeing
cycles of productivity
individual creativity and energy

persona the energy one may have towards another

my whole life i have binged on drugs food men
now i binge on this work i love to do
this is another personality trait
i have come to recognize

with the persona i feel i have a way with people

Enlighten Me

Smoking synthetic pot, incense, or K2; was what I believed helped wean me off the other drugs as a transition from an extremely addictive personality to a purging of sorts. I learned about myself in this specific era in ways I never took the time to before. I was observing myself and I learned what my likes and dislikes were. I began to identify different mannerisms as I got to know who I was becoming. A new person.

Some of the side effects from smoking synthetic pot were an uncontrolled shaking in my legs and feet and little tremors that stemmed from different thought patterns. Bingeing was an unhealthy cycle that manifested in different ways in different seasons of my life.

Binge eating is usually characterized by fast uncontrolled eating, which can be detrimental to metabolism and heart health. In this case the bingeing was not isolated to eating. So, if bingeing with food is characterized by fast uncontrolled eating, what then would bingeing on drugs or sex or anything for that matter be characterized as? The end result is it is all detrimental to the endurance of a healthy wholesome life, if not brought under self-control. Is gluttony sinful in your eyes? Do you justify your habits by saying any of the following:

- It's legal.
- The doctor prescribed it.
- If I'm gonna indulge in something at least it's food and not drugs.

Any Thoughts

_____
_____
_____
_____
_____
_____
_____
_____
_____
_____
_____
_____
_____
_____
_____
_____
_____
_____
_____
_____
_____
_____

C.I.T. – Report

the streets-some stronger than others
i haven't smoked good strong in about a week

had some today
i feel inspired for the first time in about a week
i appreciate zen and thank God out loud

i wrote a new C.I.T. first in a week
i analyzed situations clearer
i felt a body high after being inspired

the words they just flow much easier
i think this is what has been missing

<u>*Enlighten Me*</u>

The streets is slang for marijuana. Marijuana, pot, and streets, all have the same meaning. K2, synthetic, Mr. Nice Guy, and incense blend, all have the same meaning.

Marijuana and synthetic pot are two different types of smoke that I talk about. In this C.I.T. – *Report*, I share a short description from a journal entry of a mind escape I experienced and how I was affected by this specific smoke blend. Write your own description of how you felt during an experience of escaping your reality. Be honest with yourself and push through the barricades of self-deception.

Liberty Crouch

Any Thoughts

C.I.T. – Who What When How Why

who's it gonna be
dream with me hear me

analyze that doc while i keep progressing

OCD categories
categorizing things
dreams system of things

paranoia
always thinkin about who's watchin me

awakening God the Creator gives chance
through recollection
my desperation
what's my mission

i feel like God's been pushing my pen

<u>Enlighten Me</u>

Mentally, spiritually, and physically searching for my identity and purpose. Knowing that I am different yet often misunderstood, I didn't really know who to talk to about my true feelings. I so desired someone to just listen and counsel me without a carnal minded filter.

There is a difference between suspicion and being aware by discernment. Our Father who is in heaven, the Lord our God who created us and everything, He sees everything. At times I would sense that I was not alone even though nobody else was around. The Lord watches over us. The Lord sends His angels to protect us. I know now that the Lord my God is with me and has never left me. Fear births paranoia.

> For God has not given us a spirit of fear and timidity, but of power, love, and self-discipline.
>
> 2 Timothy 1:7 (NLT)

Liberty Crouch

Any Thoughts

C.I.T. – Hey Doc – Analyze This

i'm on my monthly
doin my herbal thing

no strange pains or mood swings
creative inspirational ways sway to thinkin

self-medicating
not taking Sandy's words
cause she don't know i'm on the herbs

loss of appetite loss of breath and a few bad nights
i'm in composure with myself
right?

been thinkin bout quitting altogether sometimes
smokin that is not my life

high blood pressure on the rise
sky high visualize

scared to eat gaining weight not for me

tourette syndrome acquired with time
tryin to let it go just noticing

nympho tendencies
dissipated under control
for now that is
i'm in control
need to see a real doc though

Liberty Crouch

Enlighten Me

On *my monthly* is referring to my menstrual cycle. *Sandy* is referring to the mental health doctor I was seeing for a long period of time. I did not let her know I was smoking marijuana and not taking all the medications she had prescribed me. Some of these medications had major side effects including weight gain amongst many other things. Some were prescribed to help control the high blood pressure issues the marijuana and smoking cigarettes contributed to.

While self-medicating partnered with self-deception, I never stopped writing my true feelings and analyzing them later in hopes to learn and grow from it.

Nympho tendencies refers to a sexual appetite for attention. *Suppressed*, and *under suppression*, does not mean healed. It only means, it's concealed.

Have you ever heard the term *Love Language*? In the world, without understanding our human nature or the love of God, things can get twisted. Now in Christ, I understand that I love quality time, words of affirmation, and touch. These are just a couple of examples of how my *Love Language* speaks. What are yours?

Any Thoughts

_____
_____
_____
_____
_____
_____
_____
_____
_____
_____
_____
_____

C.I.T. – Insight Doc

from age 13 on lithium
the list goes on

valium antipsychotics and midol
streets were a big hit too
herbal issues at the bottom of the list

from my mind to the gutter
from dreams to even better
success

i'm a survivor with a choice
make change make a difference and go further

follow the rules
no more outlaws in heaven

<u>*Enlighten Me*</u>

Lithium was the first medication I was ever prescribed. It was the start of a long list of medications prescribed throughout the years for the diagnosis of bipolar disorder. Bipolar disorder was an easy label for doctors to diagnose people with if a family member already had the diagnosis and/or they displayed signs of dramatic seemingly uncontrollable mood swings. I fit that category because it was told by my dad to the doctors early on that my mom was bipolar and her mom was bipolar, therefore that report followed me everywhere, to every doctor.

Streets means marijuana. I called it *streets* in code language because you can literally buy it off people who sell it on street corners.

I often battled with uncontrollable thought patterns. A lot of those thoughts stemmed from abandonment, rejection, and abuse issues. At some point I made a choice and decided to be a better person, whatever that was going to look like. I did not fully understand yet, nonetheless, I decided.

No more outlaws in heaven, that's kind of funny looking back close to 11 years ago now, not knowing any biblical reference at that time. Now,

I can see the meaning of it in the Scriptures. Satan fell from heaven because of his rebellious prideful attitude. He was the last outlaw to be in heaven.

> And He said to them, "I saw Satan fall like lightning from heaven.["]
>
> Luke 10:18

The Lord's commandments, now the rules I follow, consist of this:

> So I give you a new command: Love each other *deeply and fully*. Remember the ways that I have loved you, and demonstrate your love for others in those same ways. Everyone will know you as My followers if you demonstrate your love to others.
>
> John 13:34-35 (VOICE)

Any Thoughts

C.I.T. – Diagnosis

a chemical imbalance in the brain
bipolar manic depressive
OCAD obsessive compulsive addictive disorder
OCD obsessive compulsive disorder personality
sleep disorder
high blood pressure
anxiety
panic attacks
underactive thyroid
hyperactive attention deficit disorder
tourette syndrome
schizophrenic
nympho tendencies
memory loss short term and long
recovering drug addict
paranoid
super analyzer
migraines
body aches

that about sums it up... I think...
now do your job doc and work with me...

Enlighten Me

Funny story, I brought two pages of symptoms listed for my mental health doctor of everything I could think of that I had been labeled with or had experienced. The list above was only part of it. The doctor gave me even more prescription medication.

What pill can possibly heal you from sexual addiction from deep rooted trauma wounds? Looking at the above list of issues I can plainly see a perfect opportunity for Jesus to be glorified.

I went from fifteen pills a day prescribed for every little thing to zero pills a day after I met Jesus Christ who healed me from all of that.

Liberty Crouch

Any Thoughts

C.I.T. - Analyze This Doc

my legs and feet they never rest
they move to the beat
the drums in my head

so i try to listen to the flute in my mind
God sent messages there instead

a little slow at digesting the images shown
but i know i've grown

in 6 months
from 3 years

i will soon be in dreamland again
see all the nasties took my mind
captured thoughts and sold them for gold

when people talk i don't get the message like i thought

short term memory is a bitch
people reminding me of when i was amiss

scattered thoughts
wild imagination
paranoid adulterated interrogations

i get vibrations
in my lower limbs
like little tremors
messages from him

infinite Spirit has been pushin my pen
to try and keep up
the thesaurus has been my friend

Liberty Crouch

Enlighten Me

Self-soothing by shaking my legs was a way of receiving peace to my mind and body. Anxiety entertained would manifest into panic attacks. Short-term memory blocks have been a long-term effect of drug use.

The phrase *dreamland* is an expression for an escape from reality whenever pressure came to deal with painful thoughts.

The *flute sounds* were the soothing peace I experienced when my thoughts were peaceful. At times thoughts that needed to be processed, sounded like drums. Here is what I later learned in the Scriptures about taking control of my thoughts:

> For though we live in the world, we do not wage war as the world does. The weapons we fight with are not the weapons of the world. On the contrary, they have divine power to demolish strongholds. We demolish arguments and every pretension that sets itself up against the knowledge of God, and we take captive every thought to make it obedient to Christ.
>
> 2 Corinthians 10:3-5 (NIV)

Any Thoughts

_____
_____
_____
_____
_____
_____
_____
_____
_____
_____
_____
_____

C.I.T. – Memory Game

arranging pictures
transferring pictures to PC
then flash key and delete

repeat and delete
phone art even on CD and DVD
arranging my thoughts

no erasing misplacing
or against the grain

i'm growing brain cells every day
and still feel kinda dead inside
my brain

Enlighten Me

In the beginning of my journey of sobriety, creating pictures from my cell phone became a therapeutic tool to use my imagination in a healthy way. I learned how to transfer the pictures I created on my cell phone to my laptop computer, onto a flash drive, and even transfer the pictures onto a DVD to view. This new hobby was replacing bad habits and bad thought patterns. However, I still felt like something was missing in my life.

Any Thoughts

_____
_____
_____
_____
_____
_____
_____

Liberty Crouch

C.I.T. – Who's In Control

in my head what is it
that channels my brain
am i an experiment

paranoia always with me
as i tell the doc

who's the doc
who do i talk to
who will i see

as faces change shades get deeper

more thoughts than ever
the rhyme that riddles in your name

liberty - this journey
of self-discovery has taken you on
she exclaims

i'm always with you in your dreams
the messages are through your feet
calm them down and take your seat
who's the artist
back to mr. nice guy it's me
the air i breathe
always with me in a jam
last resort i am

depressed soul
crying out
the one people pretend to hear

but i see i see much
but not too much past
moving forward

who is she
she's the poet that didn't know it
the inspiration
the muse

they call her mammamia
that brings me to the ice princess

once you recognize
the character traits
and call them by their name
they change
it's not a science this game we play
as she changes
and figures out what to say

i am the one that gets you in trouble
i make your body ache
on the double

cause i'm the double
cold to the inner child
bold to the outside world

sex drugs and everything else
i'm addicted to you
don't cry out

tell the doc maybe she can help
ears pound
little vibrations concentration

the words i see them in my head

back to the muse
when i'm in trouble

Demons Release Trilogies, Book 3

which brings me to the doc

but the ice princess went to sleep
got to have strength
to make those bones ache
she exclaims

analyzation on that

liberty is the doc
mammamia is the muse
ice princess is the double

how many are there
that brain in there

the souls i speak of
3 i see
i said it before

but you never take your own advice
run scared in your head if you want
i'll find you i'm always around

one more question doc
who asks the questions

figure it out yourself
i help run this mission
crack your bones and change again
just stay away from mirrors
it's a sin
no mirrors in jail to keep you in
stretching and aligning changes
you too

talk it out that's what you do
and visit doc *L*

the one in charge more often

this continues for a bit
and continues in my ears

this is how i talk
now analyze this doc

back to fantasyland where it's safe

<u>Enlighten Me</u>

What channels my brain; meaning I was not sure of where random thoughts were coming from. *Strongholds of deception*; an escape of reality for fear of confronting the true calling that was ahead in my destiny. Fears of the unknown would create alternate escape routes in my mind.

Mr. Nice Guy is the brand name of a synthetic K2 incense smoke blend. This specific blend was later found to have hallucinogens in it. I used it in the beginning of my recovery from a lifelong drug addiction thinking it would help replace marijuana.

Liberty Crouch

Dreamland is a reference to a place of escape in my mind, when thoughts came with any level of pressure, requiring an immediate response.

Mirrors mean vanity. At times, self-torture would happen in the mirror. From picking bumps on my face to putting on excessive makeup to cover up the damage I did from picking, to even being self-critical and fault finding. Vanity is sin. Voices, thoughts, and vain imaginations all came as part of the torment I faced almost daily during the first part of my recovery. The gospel of Peace is part of the Armor of God that I now wear on my feet and so can you.

> Finally, my brethren, be strong in the Lord and in the power of His might. Put on the whole armor of God, that you may be able to stand against the wiles of the devil. For we do not wrestle against flesh and blood, but against principalities, against powers, against the rulers of the darkness of this age, against spiritual *hosts* of wickedness in the heavenly *places.* Therefore take up the whole armor of God, that you may be able to withstand in the evil day, and having done all, to stand.
>
> Stand therefore, having girded your waist with truth, having put on the breastplate of righteousness, and having shod your feet with the preparation of the gospel of peace; above all, taking the shield of faith with which you will be able to quench all the fiery darts of the wicked one. And take the helmet of salvation, and the sword of the Spirit, which is the word of God; praying always with all prayer and supplication in the Spirit, being watchful to this end with all perseverance and supplication for all the saints—and for me, that utterance may be given to me, that I may open my mouth boldly to make known the mystery of the gospel, for which I am an ambassador in chains; that in it I may speak boldly, as I ought to speak.
>
> Ephesians 6:10-20

Any Thoughts

C.I.T. – A Prayer for Papa

Creator,

Please forgive me of my sins and i thank you for this day and everything You have made.

Please make a way for my dad to find peace and contentment as i have Lord.

If i can share my joys in a way to make him happy.

And i ask for the use of another brain cell.

This one will be called *Patience*.

Amen.

Enlighten Me

Whenever you hear me refer to God as Creator, first, God is our Creator. He is the Creator of all things in heaven and on earth. And secondly, I heard my dad call God Creator and pray to the Creator. Not knowing God yet, or His name, I still recognized that there is a God. This is the One who gave me a second chance, gave me peace, a hope, and joy. I wanted the same thing for my dad. Day in and day out, my dad would be tormented by the spirits of alcohol and anger.

The Lord for sure answered my prayer and gave me an entirely new mind, the mind of Christ. This I share with my dad who still battles alcoholism and anger. Today, I have faith in God to endure with patience, this thing we call life. I walk victoriously and in patience, believing my dad will too.

- Do you believe there is a God?
- What is His name?
- Who do you pray to?
- Do you have a testimony of answered prayers?

Any Thoughts

Liberty Crouch

C.I.T. – Patience

don't think too much but think deep

that's how ya learn to get me

no more time will pass me by

sittin on the side lines
crying dying not for me

patience is a virtue
no disguising it

backbone composure keep cool

self-control is where it's at
moderation will be tranquil

gentle souls walk away
step back and rejuvenate

Enlighten Me

Figurative speech combined with metaphoric examples of literal situations, is what I now know to be a prophetic gift that seers have, often misunderstood by others. I recall many times I sat back and watched others participate in life while I was paralyzed with fear. Patience is a fruit of the Holy Spirit. The Lord activated that gift as I matured in faith. Read Galatians 5:22-23. Write the 9 fruits of the Spirit and circle the ones you see are activated in your life this season.

> But the fruit of the Spirit is love, joy, peace, longsuffering, kindness, goodness, faithfulness, gentleness, self-control. Against such there is no law.
>
> Galatians 5:22-23

Any Thoughts

C.I.T. – The Language of the Mayans

communication
articulate
conversation
for the interchanging

language of the Mayans
do you hear what i hear

magical tones
mysterious almost
enchanting wind chimes
play that song i like

arts and science can't predict
the calendar
or the culture

knowledge and lifestyles good chance
habit grounding folk ways
how astounding today
when will it change

Enlighten Me

God speaks to each of us in a language that we can understand. As we grow, change, transition, and become transformed into His image, the language we understand changes. The Lord knows how to speak to each of us at any given time and season of life. The Truth is revealed by His Spirit. Native American Indian beliefs were spoken by my dad often. I spoke what I heard my dad speak. In life we do, we tend to parrot the things we hear.

["]For I have not spoken on My own *authority;* but the Father who sent Me gave Me a command, what I should say and what I should speak. And I know that His command is everlasting life. Therefore, whatever I speak, just as the Father has told Me, so I speak."

John 12:49-50

So Jesus answered them by saying, "I assure you *and* most solemnly say to you, the Son can do nothing of Himself [of His own accord], unless it is something He sees the Father doing; for whatever things the Father does, the Son [in His turn] also does in the same way.["]

John 5:19 (AMP)

Any Thoughts

_____
_____
_____
_____
_____
_____
_____
_____
_____
_____
_____
_____
_____
_____
_____
_____
_____
_____
_____
_____

Liberty Crouch

C.I.T. – Sambrina the Spirit Dog

wind changes
wind chimes
that Mayan's song but faster
she growls and runs past
who is out there this time
she snarls and growls
but nowhere to be found

only the clouds and the mist

who bestoweth
upon this sanctuary
she growls
the protector

protecting her territory
brave and strong night after night
house to house
mountain to valley

the mist
as she travels the distance

Enlighten Me

Sambrina was my dad's great Pyrenees dog that lived on the mountain with us. "The Great Pyrenees is a large, thickly coated, and immensely powerful working dog bred to deter sheep-stealing wolves and other predators on snowy mountaintops. Pyrenees today are mellow companions and vigilant guardians of home and family."[1]

Any Thoughts

_____
_____
_____
_____
_____
_____

---

[1] https://www.akc.org/dog-breeds/great-pyrenees/ (retrieved 5/27/21)

C.I.T. – Get Smoked

smokin is gettin old
thinkin about just
quitting altogether

bein bold

big step for a smoker
stop smokin you're gettin old

the breaths i take
are takin my breath away

the only thing goin on is insane
thought i'd quit smokin the day i die

come to find out that day has arrived

die in time time is up

quit while you're ahead
don't wait till you're dead

Enlighten Me

After a lifelong addiction to nicotine beginning around age 12, I was finally tired of this heavy burden and I was open to receive healing in this area of my life. I once heard that the definition of *insanity* is doing the same thing over and over expecting a different result. Dying to my own selfish desire of smoking cigarettes was the beginning of the end of that addiction.

Any Thoughts

_____
_____
_____
_____
_____
_____
_____

Liberty Crouch

C.I.T. – Messages

don't forget the mission at hand
keep your path
don't get lost along the way
who will i be today

she changes
and her mind deranges
messages sent from strange places
and above spaces

get spacey
air headed like crazy

take a rest and revitalize

see it's time check the message

Enlighten Me

Staying focused on the vision of hope that kept me going was a daily choice. It seemed like I had help to do so even when nobody was around. Medication prescribed by the doctor and smoking synthetic pot along with the occasional marijuana, challenged me to focus. There were times I had to take many breaks to rest and regain focus.

Have you ever come to the place in your mind, when you have realized that the addiction you thought was helping you cope with something, really was preventing you from moving forward towards the goals you really wanted to achieve for yourself? What is the *message* that keeps you grounded?

Any Thoughts

_____
_____
_____
_____
_____
_____

C.I.T. - I am an Artist of a New Breed

a poet
a divine spirit

with an indefinite purpose
from a seed

planted in my soul hard to read
hard to understand

rantings unworldly legacy of jolted
new breed of me

can't you feel see
and breathe the things that i need

can't you see what i see

i see me an artist of a new breed
dreamin schemin
findin any way
to make me believe and

words lost and memories found
transformations and pain
goin around and around
do you hear what i speak
poetic license do i need

a role model
i think not

a leader with no followers
a sitcom with no listeners

the words that i speak
an angel with one wing

fly with me as i sing
that song that nobody's hearing

i am an artist of a new breed

so even walk with me it's endearing

Enlighten Me

The Word of God tells us in Jeremiah 1:5 and Psalm 139:13-18, that God knew us even before we were formed in our mother's womb. A *divine spirit* is a reference to the Holy Spirit living within me. I had a newfound interest in writing free verse poetry, although not yet confident of who I was, but aware that others found me peculiar. *An angel with one wing* is symbolic of a person of destiny limited by lack of knowledge.

> "Before I formed you in the womb I knew you [and approved of you as My chosen instrument], And before you were born I consecrated you [to Myself as My own]; I have appointed you as a prophet to the nations."
>
> Jeremiah 1:5 (AMP)

For You formed my innermost parts; You knit me [together] in my mother's womb.

Liberty Crouch

I will give thanks *and* praise to You, for I am fearfully and wonderfully made; Wonderful are Your works, And my soul knows it very well.

My frame was not hidden from You, When I was being formed in secret, And intricately *and* skillfully formed [as if embroidered with many colors] in the depths of the earth.

Your eyes have seen my unformed substance; And in Your book were all written The days that were appointed *for me*, When as yet there was not one of them [even taking shape].

How precious also are Your thoughts to me, O God! How vast is the sum of them!

If I could count them, they would outnumber the sand. When I awake, I am still with You.

Psalm 139:13-18 (AMP)

Any Thoughts

_____
_____
_____
_____
_____
_____
_____
_____
_____
_____
_____
_____
_____
_____
_____
_____
_____
_____

C.I.T. - Similes, Metaphors, Haiku

so what's this i do
feel free to join

open your mind be free with me

mythology read no TV
necessary
turn it off and listen to me

so what's this i do

try to school you never deceive trick or fool you
see what's out there come alive

inspire
no big mystery

<u>*Enlighten Me*</u>

Calling attention to different forms of expressive writing, in other words, *read between the lines*. Not a bunch of gibberish but rather hidden in plain sight, trying to express the thoughts in my head, yet concealing some through different forms of poetry out of paranoia.

A *simile* is a figure of speech that compares two different things in an interesting way. A *metaphor* is a figure of speech in which a word or phrase is applied to an object or action to which it is not literally applicable, a figurative expression. A *haiku* is an unrhymed poetic form consisting of 17 syllables arranged in three lines of 5, 7, and 5 syllables, separately or individually and in the order already mentioned. It is used when enumerating two or more items or facts that refer back to a previous statement.

<u>*Any Thoughts*</u>

_____
_____
_____
_____

Liberty Crouch

C.I.T. – The Perfect Man

he will hear me when i speak
in tongues if need be

he will hold me throughout the day
and be supportive all the way

he will be from the earth
but not corrupted by the world

my perfect man

he will conquer and overcome anything in his path
and adapt

he will surprise me often
and have positive around him

he will be thoughtful
and give thought to my world

when he asks me to see the sunrise
i know it will be him
he will have the seven virtues of life
and we'll work together in paradise

happiness for eternity
with our Creator

the perfect man

Enlighten Me

Throughout my life, the many men, relationships, and such, not one was the perfect man. But I held onto hope that one day I would meet the perfect man, the man of my dreams. And most recently I did marry the perfect man. True, nobody is perfect but One, and that's Jesus Christ. However, I do believe I found my perfect match. He meets the description I wrote about so many years ago.

Any Thoughts

Liberty Crouch

C.I.T. – Hide and Seek

this game my mind plays
tricks and tricked out ways

see i can be confined to an area
and in minutes
i can lose my mind
or just can't find it

lighters phones pens amiss
hide and seek so we do it again

try to keep up with my friends

referring to me
who am i now
who do you see

hide and seek
hide it from liberty

never get bored with all the games in my head
hide and seek help me find
dull moments don't exist
cause i'm always missing

you're it

<u>Enlighten Me</u>

Confusion and rebellion are unhealthy. They partner with the author of confusion and the father of lies, to keep you scattered and running aimlessly, beating the wind with your fists, getting nowhere and left feeling exhausted.

Any Thoughts

Liberty Crouch

C.I.T. – Many Men

men of many
shapes and races

same dude different faces

loyalty is what i expect
respect is what's next

i'm all about the virtues
i'm viewing you

look him in the eye
hold his hands so he can cry

still alive
who that guy
big truck big talk
daydreaming stunning
the skinny one

honey i need a hand
who him
eighteen wheels
and not enough time
that guy

what about the one in the pen
serving time inside

cause of the crime
were still surviving

chocolatier outta
this picture for now
we're not done
with the movie yet

oh, there's more

see i
tend to get in where i fit in
and that with many men

i dig chicks
but i don't get them
so, my friends many men

they've all taught me lessons
i just pray for a partner
the perfect man
one i can depend on
he will have my back

be on time and not corrupt
have patience with me
and be my ear
and shoulder most of all

Enlighten Me

How can the *same dude have different faces*? It seemed as if the same type of personality existed in many of the men I dated. Familiar spirits are demonic spirits birthed from rebellion, pride, fear, and other ungodly beliefs that can transfer from one soul to another soul that have a common ground such as these mentioned.

Research the biblical definitions of *transference of spirits* and *familiar spirits* on your own. Then it will make more sense to you and you will grow in the knowledge of the Lord.

I am literally talking about four different men who I had relationships with and gave them nicknames here to protect their identity. In these times I didn't pursue friendships with women only relationships with men. Every one of these men were not Christians and every one of these men were in rebellion against God. The Lord said in the Scriptures that rebellion is as bad as the sin of witchcraft.

> "For rebellion is as [serious as] the sin of divination (fortune-telling), And disobedience is as [serious as] false religion and idolatry. Because you have rejected the word of the Lord, He also has rejected you as king."
>
> 1 Samuel 15:23 (AMP)

Any Thoughts

_____
_____
_____
_____
_____
_____
_____
_____
_____
_____

C.I.T. – More to Frank Than Meets the Eye

screws loose and all screwed up
now i'm starting books from the back to the front

meet up in the air somewhere
from the beginning as long as you start from there

or is it here
hear what
where

from then to now

look at your progress
or digress

which is less

and more good aura to flow

spirit canyons in my ear
i also hear the language of the Mayans

<u>*Enlighten Me*</u>

Frank is an abbreviation in the C.I.T., *Frankenstein I Am* from *Book One*. The internal *issues* of scars were much deeper than the scars on the outside of my body. The trauma wounds of a lifetime were the scars of my soul. The *soul* is made up of the mind, will, and emotions.

Starting books from the back to the front is describing the way I literally started writing in my journal about halfway through the book. One day I began to write in my journal, but it just so happened to have been upside down. I placed a marker in the book when I finished with that entry. When I picked it up again, I continued to write in that direction. By the time I realized it, I had taken a literal turn in my journal and the book was almost full, so I decided to keep going in that direction. Long story short, half of the journaling in that book is read normally from left to right but then there comes the page when I started writing the other way. So in order to continue reading, the book has to be turned over, as if it were upside down.

Any Thoughts

Liberty Crouch

C.I.T. – Pharmaceutical Schemes

the streets
the means

i write about it
the man with a plan

looks like paper and a pen
scripts i speak
where's the choice for me

the streets still in my mind
but i put it to the sideline

but what i really crave
just to do a line
on my mind

but instead i give CVS my money

Enlighten Me

The *streets* is marijuana. The *means* is not referring to money but rather the means towards a stable legal way of thinking and living by taking prescribed medications from my psychiatrist. I fought through many temptations of going back to hard drugs but pushed through them and gave my money to the pharmacy for prescriptions instead.

Any Thoughts

_____
_____
_____
_____
_____
_____
_____

C.I.T. - Veins

i see my veins they're callin

it's an illusion
but the delusion

of the mind
needs to find

out why
i keep looking at my veins
they're perfect again
all the confusion
sets in and manipulates

the mind to think it'll be fine
just one more time

i cry
what are you doin

why take steps back just to find
nothing changed same games
mind fucks and head blame

why play and get setback
back in time
there's no time

but my veins they're calling me
sayin everything will be fine

as i look at the tracks

and say just once more
in my mind it's hard to find
that safe place
the right door

i was given another chance
don't give up now

close your eyes
look no more

paranoia sets in call a friend

someone who will
get that vein fill

as i wait anticipate
nothing greater
from what i remember

one more shot
that head change
that's what i crave

that body tingle
get fucked up and turn
bilingual

it's a mind game
deceive believe

what you want to
hear feel say
what ya want to

it's my game
i can do what i want to
my veins speak louder than you

it's fading out
i can't hear
the importance of it now

emotions run deep
deep as the craving that seeps
through my mind and
through my veins you see

what about dreams
can conquer fears any day
who's to say
you'll get another chance

fuck it up now if you want to
today may not bring tomorrow

listen as i speak

a flash of today's paper
in my cranium
as i turn and walk away

Liberty Crouch

Enlighten Me

When temptation came, I found myself looking at the veins in my arms. *Soul ties* can be made between any person, place, or thing that connects you or knits you together. An *ungodly soul tie* was made when I repeatedly used a needle to inject chemicals into my arms.

This C.I.T. is the conversation that was going on in my head, a literal battle of the mind. Kind of like Jiminy Cricket on one side and satan on the other, pulling me back and forth from Hope to temptation. I wrestled with the ideas of how shooting meth into my veins made me feel in the past and realizing that if I did that again even once more, I could die. I had a quick vision of seeing my name in an obituary in *Today's Newspaper*. That is when I made the choice to follow Hope and not follow death.

Any Thoughts

_____
_____
_____
_____
_____
_____
_____
_____
_____
_____
_____
_____
_____
_____
_____
_____

Demons Release Trilogies, Book 3

C.I.T. – Para What

the spirit dog barks
mysteriously

growls and runs after
the things that i hear

paranoia in the woods
in the air out there

the trees they whisper to me

what do you see
what do you hear

runnin scared out there
and in my mind

channels processing thoughts
it's a set up
a scheme

a detour of my dreams
that's what i'm thinking

and nobody around to help me

reach out

Enlighten Me

The sense of finally wanting help emotionally but feeling that I have nobody to talk to. Bound by fear; isolation was the prison I was living in my mind. I didn't know who I could talk to about my true thoughts and feelings without being judged, condemned, or put away in a mental ward, so I wrote in my journals. Paranoia was a long-term side effect from using drugs. Paranoia and fear are one in the same. Here is the Truth that will set you free if you believe. Meditate on this:

> For God did not give us a spirit of timidity *or* cowardice *or* fear, but [He has given us a spirit] of power and of love and of sound judgment *and* personal discipline [abilities that result in a calm, well-balanced mind and self-control].
>
> 2 Timothy 1:7 (AMP)

Any Thoughts

_____
_____
_____
_____
_____

C.I.T. – The Urge

it's real
overtaking minds

making choices hard to find

out what's real
the urge

so strong the abuse

what to do
who to tell
all alone in this hell

this hell is in my head
and in my soul

makes me wonder
will the urge ever get away from me?

or just take me
the urge is real
captivates and manipulates

this is how i feel

so i write
i barely got through this one
just barely

it was tough
anxiety body aches shakes cold chills

and to think
if it would've happened

what it would be like afterwards
aftermath is worse

Enlighten Me

This was an actual incident of being so tempted into relapsing and the true emotional experiences I literally walked through during the waves of withdrawal effects from meth.

I knew that my decision to abstain from cocaine and meth and the withdrawal effects that come with it, even as bad as they were, would be better for me in the long run, than the effects of doing meth continually then coming down from a high with no more drugs to do.

I say this because it would be a hopeless downward spiral if I didn't complete this withdrawal stage. Withdrawing from methamphetamines comes in waves of physical pain, mental anguish, delusions, and distress just to name a few, and lasted days on end, even for many months.

Any Thoughts

C.I.T. - Characteristics & Traits

characteristic
distinguished eccentric
emblematic exclusive individual

individualistic
idiosyncratic

as i lay down on my couch and be my own doc
i super analyze the things around me

i get a stuffy nose at night
i sing by myself

subliminally i make actions and reactions and premonitions
on health and issues around

people don't get me or is it
i don't get people

i talk too much and too loud at times
but in my mind
it seems it comes out appropriate
belonging deserved
fit useful

get fingers on and put your hands on

me the nympho the freak
the one that sets the cravings for me

schizophrenic
skittish
changeable dizzy
edgy and i must confess
i'm a whim sickle at best

paranoia it always comes
can't run from it just be professional

the roosters crow
count how many

hunting season
crows squawk

she aligns and signs
and brings zen to her
closer to her

senses be professional at all times
think like they think
in that paranoid mind

signs it in her head
don't forget to check the dates
time is coming those gates

these are just some of my characteristics & traits
besides the fact i talk
to myself and everyone around me

studio audience
don't clown me

Liberty Crouch

Enlighten Me

Keep in mind, these C.I.T.s are not in any chronological order. At some point in my recovery from methamphetamines I began to take note of my personality and characteristics.

Living with my dad, who had many cats, a lot of dust, and cobwebs throughout his house, contributed to my allergies and sinus issues. One effect being a stuffy nose. To top it off, we lived on the top of a literal mountain full of trees, plants, flowers, and pollen.

My social skills were not socially accepted per say, so whenever I had a thought, I just spoke it without any filter, self-control, any inclination of timing, nor courtesy for others. Whenever I was fearful in a circumstance or setting paranoia came. I tried to hide those feelings so that's what *be professional* means. I would talk myself out of having full blown panic attacks when I could catch it early on.

Trying to figure life out and adapt to my surroundings rather than live in my past, became my new way of maintaining peace within myself. I became ever so mindful of the end times coming and my hope of having an eternal life with God in heaven when the end does come, *heaven's gates*.

Any Thoughts

_____
_____
_____
_____
_____
_____
_____
_____
_____
_____

C.I.T. – Mission

save a life live a life mission

a journey of self-discovery on a mission to save lives for a cause
to help learn about bipolarism in generations and to keep kids off drugs
family history is an exploration
travel with me if you dare

this was a chance from God
cause my time here has been up

gotta prove to myself
that i can help myself and those around me on this mission

save a life live a life

Enlighten Me

We are now closing one chapter and about to open the next. *Mission* is another word for the *vision* in my heart. Having a sense that everything around me was about to radically change like I've never known before.

> See to it that you do not refuse him who speaks... he has promised, "Once more I will shake not only the earth but also the heavens." The words "once more" indicate the removing of what can be shaken—that is, created things—so that what cannot be shaken may remain.
>
> Hebrews 12:25-27 (NIV)

All the many tests and trials that I have been through even until now; are used for the benefit of others, to comfort others in similar experiences, and to help others see the Hope of Glory that is at work in me, in order that they too may know the mercy that awaits them through the grace of God, Jesus Christ our Sovereign Lord.

> Praise be to the God and Father of our Lord Jesus Christ, the Father of compassion and the God of all comfort, who comforts us in all our troubles, so that we can comfort those in any trouble with the comfort we ourselves receive from God. For just as we

share abundantly in the sufferings of Christ, so also our comfort abounds through Christ. If we are distressed, it is for your comfort and salvation; if we are comforted, it is for your comfort, which produces in you patient endurance of the same sufferings we suffer. And our hope for you is firm, because we know that just as you share in our sufferings, so also you share in our comfort.

We do not want you to be uninformed, brothers and sisters, about the troubles we experienced in the province of Asia. We were under great pressure, far beyond our ability to endure, so that we despaired of life itself. Indeed, we felt we had received the sentence of death. But this happened that we might not rely on ourselves but on God, who raises the dead. He has delivered us from such a deadly peril, and he will deliver us again. On him we have set our hope that he will continue to deliver us, as you help us by your prayers. Then many will give thanks on our behalf for the gracious favor granted us in answer to the prayers of many.

2 Corinthians 1:3-11 (NIV)

<u>Any Thoughts</u>

_____
_____
_____
_____
_____
_____
_____
_____
_____
_____
_____
_____

Part II – The Mission

Phone Art: What Do *You* See?
Save a Life, Live a Life
Mission: The Sacrificial Offering
of Love Poured Out

Biblical Perspective: For a long time now—to this very day—you have not deserted your fellow Israelites but have carried out the **MISSION** the Lord your God gave you.

Joshua 22:3 (NIV, emphasis mine)

Part II – The Mission

Logical Evidence is from the mind of intellectual reasoning, and tangible proof of generational cycles from the world's perspective through physical evidence.

As you begin to see and hear the voices of the world in this second chapter, through the original scanned reports and words written on the pages within this specific chapter; remember what these voices and thoughts sound like.

You will be presented in the following and final chapter of this book with the Voice of a heavenly perspective and Biblical Scripture, which is the Word of God. God, who in the beginning, was the Word.

The readers of my dreams, you have a choice. I present to you the opportunity to choose and the option to choose something Greater than yourselves.

I never knew that I had something Greater to choose from, until I heard of the option that I will present to you in chapter three of this final book of the *Demons Release Trilogies*. But as for now, let us hear the many ways of the world's view by trusted advisors in the medical field together.

Please be advised that as I was seeking professional medical help, I became a living example to the doctors, therapists, and everyone around, of the power of Christ's redemptive work daily. I was being transformed in my way of thinking. I would speak of the dreams and visions I had, even concerning the writing of these books. I became a witness to the people of a Greater Power at work in me. As I continued to seek the doctors for help with my life, prescription management, and daily living assistance, from the ones that helped along the way; not only was I provided life skills, but I was to them a sense of Hope and an encouragement to their own spiritual life as well.

Remember to write your own thoughts in this book along the way, so that in the end you can gather your own tangible evidence and be able to see for yourself how the effects of generational cycles have and can affect you and your loved ones.

Any Thoughts

_____
_____
_____
_____
_____
_____
_____
_____
_____
_____
_____
_____
_____
_____
_____
_____
_____
_____

Part II – Intro to The Mission

Concluding *Part I* and opening *Part II*, you will be reading over my original copied and scanned psychiatrists, psychologists, doctors, and therapists' documents and reports from over the past few years. To protect the privacy of the named doctors, facilities, and for other obvious privacy acts, I blocked them out.

Entry1 of these documents clearly states in the last paragraph, that I may contest information used in these medical records. During my counseling session for these records to be released, I did bring to attention a few noted mistakes that bother me. In my defense, for instance, a mentioned relapse due to a failed drug test at an outpatient rehab resulted from me taking Sudafed for allergies while living with my papa and his seven cats and Great Pyrenees dog, while I was in recovery at Owl Mountain.

Also, an obvious mistake was a date that I circled. You will see it as you continue to read. The outpatient rehab services asked me the last date I used drugs. They typed 7/14/10 and then typed the discharge date from the rehab center as 7/13/10. I do admit I was addicted to the increase of energy while taking Sudafed and energy drinks, nevertheless, I am aware that this over-the-counter drug, is one of the key ingredients that is used to make meth.

Another thing that bothered me, was judgement from Dr. Sandy. She said she thought I was using because I looked skinny, was not wearing makeup, and had sores on my face. Yes, this is a common trait of many drug addicts including myself. Makeup does hide a lot of imperfections, so without makeup to hide, you could easily put someone in this character box. The picking of my face was always an issue for me until recently. Yet, acne even lingers today. I still credit my skin problems to the pharmaceutical medications and dismiss the doctor's judgement call when crediting it to a relapse of methamphetamines, even though understandable due to my history of known drug use.

Furthermore, referring back to my C.I.T.s, I've mentioned to you all from time to time about insecurities of the mind. One of mine has always and still is, weight gain. For future reference, consider eating disorders for a possible weight fluctuation, especially if the client is mentally unstable. It's not always drug related.

Question Doc?

For many years, I confided in you.

Sandy, I told you issues of my life, relied on your knowledge and understanding for years.

I even transferred offices when you transferred to other locations because I trusted you. I thought you genuinely cared.

How about I came in for my appointment and there was a doctor in your chair, but it wasn't you.

You transferred again and didn't give notice to any of your patients. I have never seen or heard from you since.

Tell me Doc, how much abandonment and trauma do think a person can handle in a lifetime from people they put their trust into?

Did you ever care?

I guess mammon got ahold of you too!

Paper and a pen, sounds like a pharmaceutical scheme.

Call me paranoid, suspicious, co-dependent; but I call you an inconsiderate *doctor*.

I lay it out for my readers here plainly because I have no shame to hold me down. I want you to know and really grasp the whole reality of my outlook regarding the *professionals*.

Liberty Crouch

I am not trying to nitpick by pointing out mistakes they have made or computer errors. I am only acknowledging there is some incorrect information that will now trail me in *my history* wherever I go.

Please understand, as I do, everyone makes mistakes. Patients are people too, with feelings and perceptions of the world and their surroundings. However, street drugs, prescription drugs for mental illnesses, and coming off any or all of these at any given time, can alter one's perception, outlook, judgement, and appearance.

Be honest about any side effects, symptoms, and problems that are going on in your daily living situation with your doctors. They only have what you are telling them, their education, and instincts to base their decisions on as they work to help you to help yourself. Without being completely honest you may not get the correct diagnosis or proper treatment.

I have to say, that I held back quite a bit about many of my symptoms for a very long time due to the *paranoia factor*, for fear of being locked up in a mental institute. So, I withheld disclosing the symptoms I was having, such as hallucinations, delusions, hearing voices, seeing shadow people, and much more. I'm telling you this now because I feel it could help someone later who may read this.

Be honest, always, regardless of fear. Fear comes from the father of lies, satan is his name. He will try to prevent you from getting the true help you really deserve.

                      Remember you're never alone, Jesus loves you, so do I.

                      Be strong, I did this for you.

Intro to Generational Cycles: The Letter from My Mom

Date: 6/23/15

Dear Liberty,

I wish I could be more helpful to you on this project. I am very proud of your successes and the upward progress toward your goals. Strange how mental illness stripped me of most of my writing abilities while it seems to have opened yours. I have found other avenues of expression as you know it must manifest somehow. My organizational skills for writing and even editing are not as they were. My memory is short, and I have difficulty concentrating much of the time. Whatever it is, I skirt through things. Skimming words like pebbles on a lake. Ripples soon gone.

I love you. Know that.
If I can help I will.
My heart is more together than my mind. L.O.L.

Hugs and Love to you,

Mom

Enlighten Me

The mention of mental illness is relevant here because my mom acknowledges a disorder that caused her psychological and behavioral disturbances with varying severities; disorders that affected her mood, thinking, and behavior. Such mental illness includes depression, anxiety disorders, schizophrenia, eating disorders, and addictive behaviors.

I can understand what she is saying here in this letter. These mental health issues were a very real concern in my own life as well. Most people experience levels of stress and anxiety and even glimpses of depression in their lifetime. But mental health issues become more of a concern when the symptoms come more frequently and are increasingly more unmanageable.

I finally became emotionally and mentally balanced when I accepted the salvation of Jesus Christ. The Word of God gave me hope, peace, and a knowing of who I am and where I am going. I made reading the Scriptures and praying to God a part of my daily mental health regimen.

Take a moment to assess your mental health condition. Be honest with yourself. The level of honesty you have with yourself, is the level of freedom you will gain.

Any Thoughts

_____
_____
_____
_____
_____
_____
_____
_____
_____
_____
_____
_____

Testimony from My Mom: Victim No More
written by Annette
Date: unknown

I am a healthy, happy, forty-two-year-old mother of three adult children, married to a man who loves and respects me and happens to also be the father of those children. I feel extremely blessed to be living in a small mountain town and doing what I love most, writing.

But it has not always been so blissful.

My bipolar disorder, also known as manic depression or a chemical imbalance in the brain, first made itself known when I was thirteen years old. My personality underwent a drastic change, causing my parents, my teachers, and the juvenile justice system a whole lot of grief. In the late 1960's and early 1970's there was not a lot known or discussed in the area of mental illness, particularly where young people were concerned. Most of the adult population viewed these children as misfits and troublemakers and treated them accordingly.

I was one of those young people, and like so many others, I left the stable environment I knew to lead a life of *sex, drugs, and rock n roll.*

Eventually, I calmed down, got married, had children, and did the *normal* family life trip.

But it did not last forever. Undiagnosed and untreated, my mental disorder surfaced after our third child. Probably triggered by a tubal ligation, the chemical imbalance showed itself in another personality change which devastated our whole family and caused us all to go our separate ways. During the twelve years that followed, I learned all about my disease. I also became a writer in the horror genre during the manic stages (under Annette S. Crouch) and lost everything I'd ever known and loved during the depressive stages. Including my ability and confidence to write.

The beginning of my treatment for manic depression was due to being hospitalized in the mid 1980's for *bizarre behavior*. What followed was a series of drugs, abuse, and a sense of being lost. If not for my mother, my children, and most of all my God, I would not be alive to write this today.

I was more than lucky; I was loved. Family and friends are important to any healthy relationship. Treatment, when deemed necessary, and counseling, are vital to someone who is diagnosed with a mental illness; whatever reason behind the problems being faced today as a society.

Drug, child, and spousal abuse are only a few of the more obvious symptoms we see on an ever-increasing scale. Suicide, particularly among teens (when certain mental illnesses first show themselves) can be prevented. We are fortunate to live in a world where there is more information and help available to those of us who suffer.

I am no longer a victim of my own body. Because of my own experience, it was possible for me to recognize the bipolar disorder in my own daughters.

With help and understanding, none of us need to be victims of this disease. When depression kicks in, I write some very powerful poetry. When my manic side shows up, I am blessed with enough energy and inspiration to fill a ream of typing paper with saleable fiction.

The most important thing I have learned through it all is that life is what you make it. Never give up hope. And true, lasting love never dies.

No victims!

Enlighten Me

In this letter, my mom refers to bipolar disorder as hers. I have a hard time with that to be honest. I have learned that there is power in your words. Now in Christ, born again I see things differently, very differently. If you do not want it, and you know a disease is crippling you or bringing a limitation to your life somehow, why would you claim it as *your* own? I can say that now, but before I got saved, I spoke just like my mom. "*My* bipolar, *my* mental illness, *my* depression," and so on.

Generational character traits can be passed down throughout generations, good or bad, blessings and curses. What we believe, turns into the words we use, then the actions we take become behaviors and eventually a lifestyle. Please take note that my mom mentions similar experiences that I have experienced, mentioned throughout the *Demons Release Trilogies* books. A couple examples are, I had a tubal ligation after my third child and my high school education stopped at the 9th grade also.

I appreciate the transparency of this letter and my mom's willingness to share her life so that others may learn and grow from it. I love how she powerfully stands firm in her encouraging statement, "Never give up hope. And true, lasting love never dies. No victims!"

I am proud to say that my mom has been off psych meds and street drugs for so many years and she is happily married. She is an honor student in college pursuing her dreams and has helped so many people overcome through the testimonies she shares from her own life of overcoming.

My mom has been one of my biggest fans as I created these books. She never stopped believing in me and has helped with many editing critiques to keep me on track. My mom is like super woman. She bounces back and never stays down. I thank God for her.

What similar experiences have you gone through parallel to your previous generations? What else caught your attention in this letter?

Liberty Crouch

Any Thoughts

Mom's Doctor Report - 1

FROM:  M.D.
Asheville, NC

RE: CROUCH, ANNETTE S.

SPECIALIST NUMBER:

PSYCHIATRIC EVALUATION

DATE OF EVALUATION: June 23, 1999

GENERAL OBSERVATIONS: This 42-year-old divorced white female is punctual for the appointment, in fact arrives 1/2 hour early, accompanied by male friend. She reports that she does possess valid driver's license and a vehicle. She gives her height at 5'2", her current weight at 140 pounds, noting that weight is essentially stable. She assumes erect and normal posture, gait is unremarkable. While there are no involuntary movements, there is gross evidence of fidgetiness and tension in the interview from start to finish. She has an admixture of cooperation in attitude with resistance and defensiveness. She is dressed in casual clothing that appears clean, shows evidence of fair hygiene.

PRESENT ILLNESS: The claimant describes at age 13 onset of trouble with mood disorder, which through the years has received varying diagnosis, but ultimately has come to be stated as bipolar disorder. She can here today recall two significant manic episodes in which she was psychotic, but most abnormal phases have found her depressed in her mood, previously suicidal but not at this time. She has worked at various jobs in her adult lifetime, seems to have preferred restaurant cook occupation, reports her longest job tenure was 2 years. She last worked in 1998, approximately 1 year ago, and has since been attending technical school courses in office operations, especially focused on computer, and notes she has a PC at home. History includes probably 4 psychiatric hospitalizations, all of them are reported as on an involuntary commitment basis, two of them in California, and probably two of them in Oregon as well. She had several year affiliation with Mental Health Centers in California and Oregon, but since arriving in western North Carolina approximately 3 years ago, she is not affiliated. She states openly that this session today causes her to feel resistant, because of the process involving recall. Other than that, she has been over it before and does not wish to recall or feel again. She notes that she's under the general medical care of a Dr. in Waynesville, who prescribes Nasacort and Claritin-D for sinus problems, and that she's been on Paxil

Mom's Doctor Report – 2

June 20, 1999　　　　　　　RE: CROUCH, ANNETTE S.
Page 2

currently prescribed by him 20 mg tabs, 2 daily over the past approximately 5 years. This plus the move here from western U.S. is given credit for providing her some stability in her mood and behavior over at least these last 3 years. She states that she's very neutral in her mood at this time, has no experience with the manic phase such as racing thoughts, ideas of grandiosity, impulsive behaviors, or significant sleep problems. At the same time, does not become violent when she feels accosted by violent behaviors from others, nor is she mired in depression with suicidal thoughts. She has trouble trusting people unless and until she gets to know them. She cites her goals as "to be able to stick with things". She also reports a previous drug abuse history, especially featuring illicit substances, predominantly speed, but also crank and heroin, states she's been totally abstinent for indefinite period of time. She denies alcohol use has been problematic, notes she may only occasionally have a drink. Her sleep is described as normal for her, her appetite also within normal limits. The claimant notes finally that she's here for mandated review of Disability status which she's qualified for for unknown number of years.

PERSONAL AND FAMILY HISTORY: She is originally a Californian, spent a good amount of time in her life in Oregon, also Arizona, and mentions Texas as well, has been in this area for 3 years. Her family of origin history is very complicated, so much so that I cannot repeat it here, but this is described aptly in a previous report supplied by DDS. She remains close to her adoptive parents to this day, and to one biological sister. She reports a 9th grade education, dropout, then obtaining G.E.D. and is currently enrolled in "college" courses. She says that she along with her husband at the time enlisted in the U.S. Army, year unknown, spent 4 weeks there, believes she received honorable discharge, though she mentions here that she has always had trouble with authority and did so in the service as well. She feels the Army lied to her in attracting her and her husband to enlist. She was married for the first time at age 16, divorced after 3 years and had no children. Her second marriage undertaken at age 20, produced three children, the oldest is a son and the other two are daughters. These children are reported as reared partly by her, partly by her ex-husband, partly by the children's grandparents. Currently, she rents a small house, has two pet cats.

The claimant gives a positive response when asked about a family history of mental illness, describing grandmother as a hypochondriac who lived to be age 90, her mother "kind of schizophrenic", and she has two daughters with mental problems, one diagnosed with bipolar disorder.

Mom's Doctor Report - 3

June 20, 1999 RE: CROUCH, ANNETTE S.
Page 3

Substance abuse history is noted above, she denies any formal treatment for drug or alcohol abuse.

MEDICAL/SURGICAL HISTORY: Essentially benign, as she notes tubal ligation with incidental appendectomy.

ACTIVITIES OF DAILY LIFE: She spends considerable time at the computer checking e-mail. She feeds the birds outdoors and her own cat, tends to drink coffee, eat fairly normally, is bothered frequently, especially in this season, by sinus difficulties. She reports herself as a serious housekeeper, keeping cleanliness about her, enjoying a small garden with vegetables and flowers. She enjoys writing and states that she's had a writing experience in which she "used to get published a lot," implying this is not done at the present time, but she does note that she has had to do less of writing short stories and novels, spends more time writing poetry nowadays. She attends a health club 3 times weekly, is "sort of" physically active. She is a social loner which she states is a life-long trait, does see her daughter and daughter's two sons frequently while they are in this area for the Summer. She does little reading, does pay attention to news. She enjoys rock music. She reports having quit cigarette smoking 2-1/2 years ago.

MENTAL STATUS EXAMINATION:
Attitude and behavior: She is in good contact with reality throughout the session, shows a slightly subdued psychomotor activity level, and speaks at some points in barely audible voice. She has serious, defensive demeanor, but is not overtly angry, does in her way try to be cooperative. She has no demonstration of loss of impulse control. Her motivation appears to be positive for maintaining status quo, that is being consistent in mood, and removed from stress that she has experienced to great extent in her life earlier.

Stream of mental activity: Shows only fair spontaneity, but she can organize her thinking, use logic, shows no pressured speech. There is no blocking or thought inhibition really.

Mental trend and thought content: Devoid of any psychotic ideations. She is suspicious of other people and prone to not trust them, which also appears to be a life-long trait. She shows no obsessions. She denies current suicidal thoughts, describes her self-esteem as positive at this point.

Affect: Blunted, with barely covert hostility evident, no overt depressive mood tone or fear shown. She only partly trusts this interviewer, is highly anxious and fidgety throughout the session.

Liberty Crouch

Mom's Doctor Report – 4

June 20, 1999   RE: CROUCH, ANNETTE S.
Page 4

Cognition: She is correctly oriented for time, place, person, and for an understanding of why she is here.

Memory as tested through being given 5 numerals, finds her repeating these in forward order correctly, but unable to name them in reverse order. She remembers only 1 out of 3 items retained for 3 minutes. Her date of birth is given correctly, as is the presidential reversal from Clinton through Reagan.

Her fund of information as tested by naming large cities, famous people, and current newsworthy events is very adequate, more than adequate, in fact.

Her calculation is tested through subtracting serial sevens from 100, and here she's noted to proceed rapidly but to make the same mistake in subtracting 7 from 93 and getting 84, later subtracting 7 from 63 and getting 54. She can add and subtract single digits correctly.

Abstract thinking as tested through: "people in glass houses should not throw stones" is given another saying in response, "you should sweep off your own back porch".

Judgment is found to be intact.

Intellectual level here is grossly estimated at average.

Concentration is defective to minor extent, attention span minimally shortened.

SOMATIC COMPLAINTS: Are minimal other than reporting recurrent headaches, sometimes severe. She admits to good energy, preservation of body strength, normal appetite and sleep.

Functionally, this individual appears historically to have indeed experienced an early teenage onset of bipolar disorder, and apparently has the family history that can go with this. ~~frequently~~. She has had her life significantly interrupted by decompensations into at least 2 manic episodes and probably more depressive disorders, has been suicidal, has been psychotic, but in the last 3 years and since moving to this area, appears to have affiliated with local family practitioner and taking prescribed medication reliably, which currently consists only of Paxil 40 mg per day. I noted from records that she was previously noncompliant often, and objected to the use of Lithium previously. She reports managing her own finances well, living comfortably on her meager income, maintaining interests especially in writing and in computer work and in fact is taking community college courses ostensibly to use in future employment.

Demons Release Trilogies, Book 3

Any Thoughts

Liberty Crouch

Poem – Life

written by my daughter a.k.a. Pink Ice Princess Warrior
(age 9, also pg.24 *Book One*)

Life isn't the best
I'm stuck with a pest
Wish I could move out west
This morning
I found
A bird's nest
I need to get some rest

I got a big brother
Always bullying me
I wish I had someone nicer
Than he

I'm not my stepmom's maid
My dad he treats me like a slave

I wish I could slither
Like a snake right out of
This mess
I'd move in with my friend Jess

I'm tired of being like
Cinderella
I think I'll sit in the rain
With my umbrella

Enlighten Me

My daughter at age 9 expresses in the language of poetry, figuratively speaking, the hardships she was experiencing. She was living with her dad and his girlfriend at that time.

What do you hear? How would you express the hardships of your present life?

Any Thoughts

Liberty Crouch

Poem – In America
written by my daughter
Date: 4/26/16

In America, it is 2016, there's fighting.
There's killing, there's selfish, and selfless acts.
We have people screaming,
"Stop the Racism,"
Yet we are killing each other over disrespect.
We have officers screaming,
"Stop Put Your Hands Up,"
Yet they still shoot.
In America,
we have teenaged girls:
Selling their bodies, exposing themselves,
All because, "Daddy never came back to raise them."
In America,
we have presidents saying,
"They'll Give Us Better."
Yet they've given us nothing but words,
That turn into lies.
In America,
we have children being born with Smart Phones,
Laptops,
I pods,
And Xboxes,
Yet they are told to, "Grow Up."
In America,
we have children being raised around drug dealers,
Thieves,
Abusers,
Mentally and physically,
Then when asked, later in life,

"Why?"
"Why Did You Do It?"
THEY DON'T KNOW ANY BETTER
In America,
Where we are told,
"Go Out and Get Your Education."
Yet the dummies and thieves are rich,
And our scholars,
Are broke,
And depressed.
In America,
When we have teenagers,
Killing themselves,
Not even knowing,
It gets better,
You haven't even experienced real "life",
All over how they are momentarily feeling,
Their hormones,
In America,
Where we have people,
People thinking this was a better way?
Thinking they could become anyone,
When there is a society that secretly hates you,
Yet smiles in your face,
When we have children battling,
These terrible battles, battles in their head,
They'll never know it gets better.
So, when asked,
In America,
"Why do they say this is such a great place?"
I'll never know,
People here,
Only love themselves,
And their money.

Liberty Crouch

Enlighten Me

What choices we make today have lasting effects on future generations. I remember not knowing how to parent my three children, therefore buying material objects for my kids to show them that I loved them. I remember using the television for a babysitter. I remember allowing my children to play video games that encouraged murder, auto theft, and vulgar language to say the least. And do I think that I may have contributed to society the way my daughter describes? Most definitely, yes. How brutally honest.

Today, my daughter is a law student in college and is pursuing her passion of justice as a criminal lawyer. Today, my daughter follows Jesus Christ as her Lord and Savior. Today, I am overwhelmed with gratitude as I see the favor of God on her life. This mighty young lady truly stands for Justice and Truth.

Any Thoughts

Journal Entry:
Counseling Session Prior to the Release of My Personal Medical Records

Today is Sunday, June 2, 2013. I've been fasting every Sunday since January 13th, except for my papa's birthday lunch, which was on Sunday April 14th; the day my family came to celebrate my baptism; and this past Mother's Day. Today I fast for God Almighty's love to surround my family, friends, and loved ones, to build my faith never-ending, everlasting, and for mind strength to come like never before, in order to complete this mission He has created me for.

In order for me to complete this trilogy, I will be going for a counseling appointment with my therapist and another doctor at the mental health place to collect copies of all documented history from my psychiatrists, psychologists, and others that have helped me along the way. The counseling is required so that if I have questions or *just in case* I get disturbed in any way from bringing up my past, the doctors' analyzations, notes, and such, I won't go into shock or shut down by myself. Pretty much, they will help me process the information.

> Wise strategy is necessary to wage war,
> and with many astute advisers
> you'll see the path to victory more clearly.
> Proverbs 26:6 (TPT)

I'm not sure how long of a session or how emotional it may be. I'm preparing mentally with constant prayer from myself and others.

I know God has never left me and certainly will not leave me stranded now or ever. All the information that I will gather from the doctors from over the years, will soon come to the surface to fulfill its purpose. This I know. The mind strength, faith, and love above all, will keep me grounded as I walk through the valley of the shadow of death, I will fear no evil.

I do pray that if any doors be opened during these times, that my Helper, Holy Ghost Spirit, come swiftly and fill me up with these things that I've asked and close the doors so that no evil can come back in. Jesus Christ dwells within me.

Liberty Crouch

I was guided by just a thought, an *impression,* that led me to start reading the Book of Isaiah. Prayers were already beginning to be answered. I got here:

> Fear not, for I *am* with you;
> Be not dismayed, for I *am* your God.
> I will strengthen you,
> Yes, I will help you,
> I will uphold you with My righteous right hand.'
> Isaiah 41:10

I read all the way to Isaiah chapter 45. I was so inspired by this confirmation. Isaiah 43:21 encouraged me when I heard God saying, "This people I have formed for Myself; They shall declare My praise."

These Scriptures are so personally breathtaking, the desire I hear God has for and to be in a relationship with His people. I believe Him.

Medical Records

The purpose of allowing the readers of my dreams to observe my personal medical records, is to show tangible evidence of generational history, professionally recorded. Note the similarities in the testimonies of my mom and myself and the poems from my mom and daughter.

My hope is to transparently show where I came from to who I have become, through the power of Christ Jesus' resurrected blood, in a real enough way, that you also would believe in the power of Christ Jesus and be set free from ungodly beliefs that have kept you or someone you know in bondage by wrong thinking.

As I was sorting through these records and deciding on which ones to use in this book, I labeled them with entry numbers and other footnotes to keep myself organized for the making of this chapter. Aiming for authentic transparency, I decided to keep my written thoughts on each entry for you.

At the end of this chapter, you will have an opportunity to write your overall thoughts about some noteworthy topics that stuck out to you.

Please do not hinder your own freedom by judging my journey towards freedom. Every entry I have chosen to use in this book is on purpose, from medication management to vital reports to home therapist notes. Also included are the noted history of me talking about future plans to write a book; making pictures with my cell phone; and important notes where you can obviously see some errors from doctors who probably just didn't take their time to read the previous notes before adding theirs to it.

As you read through my dramatic medical and psychological history, keep in mind, I was a drug addict shooting meth into my veins, using cocaine and other drugs to escape a painful reality. Over a period of time, freedom was birth from within me. I now walk in a freedom that so many only dream of. Understand, it was the Lord our God who loved me first, even while I was still a sinner. He brought me through *that* darkness. He lead me to the Light, not just for my own freedom, but so that you can see and believe it is possible for you too.

> But God demonstrates His own love toward us, in that while we were still sinners, Christ died for us.
>
> Romans 5:8

> But you *are* a chosen generation, a royal priesthood, a holy nation, His own special people, that you may proclaim the praises of Him who called you out of darkness into His marvelous light;
>
> 1 Peter 2:9

> Now it was not written for his sake alone that it was imputed to him, but also for us. It shall be imputed to us who believe in Him who raised up Jesus our Lord from the dead, who was delivered up because of our offenses, and was raised because of our justification.
>
> Romans 4:23-25

I stand today victorious over all the mental diagnoses mentioned in these reports. I stand victorious over all substance abuse issues mentioned in these reports. And I stand victorious over all noted generational diagnoses and other issues mentioned in this book, even to the point of standing in the gap for the freedom of future generations. I stand knowing that my victory is because of the resurrected blood of my Savior Jesus Christ.

Any Thoughts

Entry 1 - Client Access Record Permission

Client/Parent/Guardian Record Access

Client Name: **Liberty Crouch** Record Number: _____

Instructions: This form must be completed in order for a client, parent, or legal guardian to access the client's medical record. A member of the client's professional treatment team must be present during the review. If the client receives a copy of any medical record information, including psychological evaluations, the documents must be stamped as "Client Copy".

I hereby request access to information contained in the medical record of the above named client.

I understand that a qualified professional will be present when I review the medical record to answer any questions I may have.

The professional may deny any information that would be injurious to me or to another person including physical, mental and/or emotional well being.

I further understand that I may contest information contained in the medical record. However, original documentation may not be deleted and/or altered in any way. If the primary therapist, physician, or treatment provider concurs with the correction it may be included in the medical record as a progress note.

_____   _____6/5/13_____
Signature of Client/Parent/Legal Guardian   Date Signed

_____Katie_____   _____6/5/13_____
Witness Signature   Date Signed

Liberty Crouch

Entry 2 – Note Date: 07/23/2010

[Handwritten: Entry 3 10 pages total pg 1]

Patient Name: CROUCH LIBERTY
Provider Name:
Encounter Date: <None>
Note Date: 07/23/2010

Saling Header............................:
RU: 391 , Time: 10 . 00 , Duration: 1 . 00 , Service Code: ace of Service:

GOAL: To provide an intensive clinical and functional face to face evaluation of a consumer's substance abuse and mental health conditions.

INTERVENTION: I assessed and determined whether the consumer is appropriate for and can benefit from SA IOP based on the recipient's diagnosis, presenting problems, and treatment and recovery goals. I also evaluated the consumer's level of readiness and motivation to engage in treatment and recovery goals.

OUTCOME: Issuance of a Comprehensive Clinical Assessment/PCP Lite report which includes a recommendation regarding whether the recipient meets target population criteria, and meets criteria for admission to IOP.

CONFIDENTIAL AND PRIVILEGED
This information may be protected by Federal Regulation 42 C.F.R. Re-disclosure of this information is prohibited by law without the client/legal representative's written consent. If either should request access to this information they should be referred back to our agency.

Entry 3 - Note Date: 08/09/2010 Diagnosis

Patient Name: CROUCH, LIBERTY A
Provider Name: _____ SANDY
Encounter Date: <None>
Note Date: 08/09/2010

PROPERTY OF
_____ALTH SERVICES
CONFIDENTIAL AND PRIVILIGED
This information may be protected by Federal Regulation
disclosure of this information is prohibited by
law without the client/legal representative's written
consent. If either should request access to this information
they should be referred back to our agency.

Medication Evaluation Progress Note...............:
Time: 11.00, Duration: 0.25, Service Code: _____ Place of Servi_____

CC: Medication Evaluation

HPI: I have been following this patient through the _____, center and _____. They have decided to come to _____ IS in order to continue to see me for their medication management. Unfortunately she had a relapse of Methamphetamines (I didn't know that she once had a problem with this as she never shared this with me). She states she had a two week relapse however was "shooting up" and unfortunately got an infection in her breast (location of injection). She has breast implants and will have to have them removed so she's upset by that. She detoxed at the _____ and now is going to SA-IOPT.

She saw Dr _____ at the _____ for f/u and didn't have a good experience. She is on Neurotin and it was just increased to 400mg for anxiety. Her abilify was decreased to 15mg. She is no longer on Wellbutrin and doesn't feel that it was helping her at all anyway. She says she is experiencing panic attacks without the klonopin and xanax that she used to be on, which she is off of now. She doesn't understand why she can't be on these again, as she says "I never abused those medicines." She denies SI/HI or any psychotic features.

REVIEW OF SYSTEMS:
General: See HPI
Musculoskeletal: No chronic pain issues
Neurologic: No syncopal episodes, history of stroke, seizures, vertigo or head injuries
Psychiatric: see subjective or HPI
Breasts: Infection from site of injection of meth use. States she'll have to have implants removed.

MENTAL STATUS EXAM: Caucasian female, of normal body habitus, casually dressed, and appropriately groomed, appearing as age stated. The patient makes good eye contact with conversation. Scleras are non-icteric. Mood is depressed and affect is tearful. The patient is alert and oriented x4. The patient's language is within normal limits. Speech is within normal limits particularly pertaining to rate, articulation, spontaneity, and tone. The patient's thoughts are linear and goal oriented. Insight and judgment appears to be good. No psychosis identified. Cranial nerves 2-7, as well as coordination and fine motor skills are grossly intact. No choreic or athetosis movements detected. Slight hand tremor noted. Gait is normal. Skin is acyanotic. No clubbing of digits noted.

The patient had a diagnosis of schizoaffective disorder, however in light of her recent meth use I would question that diagnosis and reclassify as bipolar disorder

DIAGNOSIS:
Axis I: Bipolar disorder type I; panic disorder (may be related to substance abuse); PTSD; methamphetamine abuse
Axis II: Borderline personality disorder
Axis III: infection in breast implant
Axis IV: problems relating to environment secondary to anxiety issues
Axis V: GAF 48

PLAN: I've explained to the patient that I'm not comfortable in light of her recent illicit drug use, using any controlled substances at this time. I will speak to _____ and see how Liberty is doing in SA-IOPT. We'll increase her dose of Abilify to 20mg which worked for her in the past, and add Vistaril 50 to 100mg q 6 hrs, prn for anxiety. She'll remain on Gabapentin 400mg tid, and Trazodone 150mg q hs. She is advised to RTC in one month for f/u.

Note: The statement made before the *Diagnosis* and the *Diagnosis Section* for the purpose of ongoing noted diagnosis entries.

Liberty Crouch

Entry 4 – Reasons for Seeking Services

Reasons for Seeking Services

Referred for assessment of: ☐ MH ☐ DD ☒ SA Problems
UDS results at intake: positive for opiates (rx)

Presenting Problems
Substance abuse
Amphetamine Dependence: Last use date: 7/14/10 when she injected meth. Daily use of 3 grams a day. She has been injecting for the last 2 months during which time she disappeared and had no contact with family. She starting using at age 29. She used for a few months, moved to Fla and was stopped for a year. When she moved back here a year ago she started using.
Nicotine Dependence: daily smoking of less than a pack.
Cocaine Dependence: Last use date: 3/3/10 when used a gram once for the first time years. Used from age 18 until 6 years ago when she realized she might lose her three children.
Mental Health
Bipolar dx is basis of SSI which she has had since 2006. Has been on medication since age 13. Panic disorder since age 12.

Precipitating Events (Why seeking services *NOW?*)
Discharged from ████████ 7/13/10 where she detoxed since 7/8/10.

What are the top three stressors in your life: DSS involvement, her sister lack of support, her dad is getting support.
Legal Issues Related to Substance Abuse:
None

General Health History

Problems and Symptoms: breast abscesses from IV drug use
Treatment: upcoming doctor's appointment

Known allergies & adverse medication reactions:
☒ None known/reported

HIV ? ☐ Yes ☐ No ☐ Unknown
Hepatitis C ☐ Yes ☐ No ☐ Unknown
Ever injected with a needle ? ☐ Yes ☒ No ☐ Unknown
Referral Made for medical care.

Ever had tuberculosis? ☐ Yes ☒ No ☐ Unknown

PROPERTY OF ████████ SERVICES
CONFIDENTIAL AND PRIVILIGED
This information may be protected by Federal Regulation 42 C.F.R. Re-disclosure of this information is prohibited by law without the client/legal representative's written consent. If either should request access to this information they should be referred back to our agency.

Mental Health Treatment History *(Please check all that apply)* ☐ None ☐ Unknown

☒ Outpatient When/Where/Who:
  Outcome: ☐ Unknown ☐ Improved ☐ No change ☐ Worse
  Treatment compliance (non-med): ☐ Unknown ☐ Poor ☐ Fair ☐ Good

☐ IOP/Partial When/Where/Who:
  Outcome: ☐ Unknown ☐ Improved ☐ No change ☐ Worse
  Treatment compliance (non-med): ☐ Unknown ☐ Poor ☐ Fair ☐ Good

☒ Inpatient/Residential When/Where/Who: In Florida   3 times the last time was 8 years ago.
  Outcome: ☐ Unknown ☒ Improved ☐ No change ☐ Worse
  Treatment compliance (non-med): ☐ Unknown ☐ Poor ☐ Fair ☒ Good

Number of psychiatric hospitalizations in the past 12 months: 0 in lifetime: 3

Additional MH Treatment History/Information:

Demons Release Trilogies, Book 3

Entry 5 – Reasons for Seeking Services

Name: Crouch, Liberty   SMC LME Client Record #

Current Psychotropic Medications	Dose	Frequency	Usually adherent?	
Zyprexa	5 mg	1 X	☒ Yes	☐ No
Abilify	5 mg	1 X	☒ Yes	☐ No
Gabapentin	300 mg	3 X	☒ Yes	☐ No
Trazadone	160 mg	BID	☒ Yes	☐ No
Hydrocodone	PRN		☒ Yes	☐ No
Ibuprofen	800 mg		☒ Yes	☐ No

Medication History:

Substance Abuse Treatment History *(Please check all that apply)*   ☐ Received No Treatment

☐ Outpatient
   When/Where/Who:
   Outcome: ☐ Unknown ☐ Improved ☐ No change ☐ Worse
   Treatment compliance (non-med): ☐ Unknown ☐ Poor ☐ Fair ☐ Good

☐ IOP/Partial
   When/Where/Who:
   Outcome: ☐ Unknown ☐ Improved ☐ No change ☐ Worse
   Treatment compliance (non-med): ☐ Unknown ☐ Poor ☐ Fair ☐ Good

☒ Inpatient/Residential
   When/Where: ▓▓▓▓▓▓▓▓▓▓▓ 7/8/10-7/13/10
   Outcome: ☐ Unknown ☒ Improved ☐ No change ☐ Worse
   Treatment compliance (non-med): ☐ Unknown ☐ Poor ☐ Fair ☒ Good

   When/Where/Who:
   Outcome: ☐ Unknown ☐ Improved ☐ No change ☐ Worse
   Treatment compliance (non-med): ☐ Unknown ☐ Poor ☐ Fair ☐ Good

- Number of substance abuse hospitalizations in the past 12 months:
- Number of substance abuse hospitalizations in lifetime:

Additional Substance Abuse Treatment History:

Is individual currently enrolled in an opioid treatment program:

Alcohol & Drug Use
☐ No current/recent use of alcohol or other drugs
☐ Current/recent use of alcohol & other drugs within normal limits
Comments:

Current/Recent Abuse Indicators
   ☐ Recurrent use resulting in major role failure
   ☐ Recurrent use in situations in which it is physically hazardous
   ☐ Recurrent substance-related legal problems
   ☐ Continued use despite causing persistent or recurrent social or interpersonal problems

Current/Recent Dependence Indicators
   ☒ Tolerance
   ☒ Withdrawal
   ☒ Substance taken in larger amounts or over longer time than intended
   ☒ Persistent desire or unsuccessful efforts to cut down or control substance use
   ☒ Great deal of time spent in activities necessary to obtain substance
   ☒ Important social, occupational, or recreational activities given up or reduced because of substance use
   ☒ Use continued despite knowledge of having persistent/recurrent physical or psychological problem

Liberty Crouch

Entry 4

Note: Date of last use 7/14/2010. Discharge date from a detox facility of 7/13/2010. Then it is also noted detoxed since 7/08/2010.

Question: How could I possibly be detoxed since 7/08 and at the same time my last noted use date here is 7/14 while I was discharged on 7/13. Also, it clearly asks if ever injected with a needle and *no* is marked as the answer, when clearly this same note states in the very first paragraph that I had been injecting for the last 2 months. You cannot be detoxed and using at the same time. You cannot be discharged from a facility while still being noted as admitted. And you clearly cannot *not ever* use a needle while still being noted as injecting. People make mistakes. Let's move on.

Any Thoughts

Entry 6 – Substance Abuse Dependence History & Relevant Family History

Name: Crouch, Liberty   SMC LME Client Record

Substance Abuse/Dependence History   ☐ No current or past substance abuse or dependence

	Substance	Method	Age 1st use	Current Frequency	Amount Current Use	Date Last Used (YYYYMMDD)
Primary	09 Methamphet	4 injection	29	4=daily use	3 grams	20100714
Secondary	02 Cocaine/Crac	2 smoking	18	0=not in past	1 gram	20100303
Tertiary	Select	Select		Select		

N.C. Modified A/ASAM Placement Level: III.7 recommended by assessor. III.3 recommended by the NEEDS but client desires a less restrictive level of treatment so will try a level II.1 IOP. If client is unable to maintain abstinence will be referred to a higher level of care.

Developmental Disabilities History:
Problems and Symptoms: None reported
Treatment:
Response to Treatment:
Attitudes about Treatment:
Factors contributing or inhibiting previous recovery:

Consumer's Supports

Ability to Care for Self
Competency Status: ☐ Minor (M)
☒ Competent Adult or Adjudicated Minor (C)
☐ Incompetent Adult (I)
☐ Unknown (U)

Primary Support Group:
Her father

Friendships and Social Supports
Two women who are sober

Recovery environment and living situation:
She just moved in with father.

Attends 12-step meetings? How often? Has a sponsor
About 6 years old

History of Abuse or Neglect   ☐ No history of abuse or neglect
Sexual abuse from her mother's roommate's father when she age 5. Her sister was also abused. Was raped by 4 or 5 guys.

Relevant Family History
Her three children are in temporary custody of DSS of her oldest 15 son who is placed with her brother. Can't see him but she can talk to him on the phone. DSS has an open case plan. The other two are with their father and she can see them when ever she wants.
She was raised by her dad. She was always been "the bi-polar black sheep of the family." She is the middle of three children. Her mother has bipolar and has had drug problem and has been clean for 10 years. They currently have contact. At some point her mother remarried to Liberty's father but then they divorced again and she is now living in Maryland. Reports her grandmother had bipolar and schizophrenia.

Highest Educational Level	
☐ None, never attended school	☐ 04 Fourth grade
☐ Kindergarten (30)	☐ 05 Fifth grade
☐ 01 First grade	☐ 06 Sixth grade
☐ 02 Second grade	☐ 07 Seventh grade
☐ 03 Third grade	☐ 08 Eighth grade
	☐ 09 Ninth grade
	☐ 10 Tenth grade

Liberty Crouch

~ 102 ~

Entry 7 – Current Mental Status

Name: Crouch, Liberty   SMC LME Client Record

☐ Other:
Risk of Harm to Self (Recent/ current)   ☐ None
☐ Suicidal thoughts ☐ Suicidal threats ☐ Suicidal plans ☒ Suicide attempts
☐ Family history of suicide ☐ Preoccupation with death Comments: about 3. 2006, 2005 and when she was 11.
History of Harm to self
☐ Suicidal threats ☐ Suicide Attempts: date: Circumstances:
Risk of Harm to Others (Recent/ current)   ☒ None
☐ Thoughts to harm others ☐ Threats to harm others ☐ Plans to harm others
☐ Attempt to harm others   Comments:

Other mental status information:

PROPERTY OF
CONFIDENTIAL AND PRIVILEGED ...SERVICES
This information may be protected by Federal Regulation 42 C.F.R. Re-disclosure of this information is prohibited by law without the client/legal representative's written consent. If either should request access to this information they should be referred back to our agency.

Other Assessment Information & Data
See NEEDS assessment.

For Women with Substance Abuse Issues:
Is this woman:
   a. Pregnant? ☐ Yes ☒ No
   b. Legal custodian of at least one child under 18 years of age? ☐ Yes ☒ No
   c. Currently seeking custody of a child under 18 years of age? ☐ Yes ☒ No
   d. Currently or recently involved with DSS? ☒ Yes ☐ No
   e. Authorized for Work First Assistance? ☐ Yes ☒ No

2) This individual's primary medical care status and needs: is currently receiving medical care.
3) This individual's child pediatric care status and needs: n/a
4) This individual's gender specific treatment needs: address women's recovery issues in group.
5) Women's child therapy status and needs: n/a
6) This individual's case management status and needs: none reported
7) This individual's transportation and housing status and needs: needs transportation temporally, will need housing in 4 months.
8) This individual's child care status and needs: n/a
9) This individual's pre-natal/pregnancy status and needs: n/a
10) What information about alcohol, tobacco and drug use, abuse and addiction and their effects on individuals and what community based program information was shared while assessing consumer? This is an SA abuse program.

DSM-IV-TR Diagnoses

Disorder	DSM-IV-TR Code	Effective Date (YYYYMMDD)
Axis I: Clinical Disorders		
1. Amphetamine Dependence	304.40	20100716
2. Cocaine Dependence	304.20	20100716
3. Bipolar Disorder, depressed	296.89	20100716
4. Panic Disorder, w/o agoraphobia	300.22	20100716
5. Nicotine Dependence	305.10	20100716
Axis II: Personality Disorders and Mental Retardation		
1. Deferred	799.9	20100716
2.		
3.		

Demons Release Trilogies, Book 3

Entry 8 – Assessment Interpretation

Name: Crouch, Liberty   SMC LME Client Record

Axis III: General Medical Conditions
1. breast abscesses
2.
3.

Axis IV: Psychosocial and Environmental Problems
☒ Problems with primary support group
   Specify: none of three children are in her care
☒ Problems related to the social environment
   Specify: needs to avoid using friends
☐ Educational Problems
   Specify:
☐ Occupational Problems
   Specify:
☐ Housing Problems
   Specify:
☐ Economic Problems
   Specify:
☐ Problems with access to health care services
   Specify:
☐ Problems related to interaction with the legal system/crime
   Specify:
☒ Other psychosocial and environmental problems
   Specify: DSS involved

Axis V: Global Assessment of Functioning (GAF)
Current GAF: 45
Highest GAF in past year:

CONFIDENTIAL AND PRIVILEGED
This information may be protected by Federal Regulation 42 C.F.R. Re-disclosure of this information is prohibited by law without the client/legal representative's written consent. If either should request access to this information they should be referred back to our agency.

Level of Care

☐	A	GAF > 70 or ASAM I
☐	B	GAF 51-70 or ASAM II.1
☒	C	GAF 31-50 or ASAM II.5
☐	D	GAF < 31

Target Population Recommendations

Adult Target Group	
☐ Mental Health	
☒ Substance Abuse	ASCDR
☐ Developmental Disability	
☐ Not in a Target Population	

Assessment Interpretation & Case Formulation

Liberty is a 31 year old white female seeking admission to SA-IOP. She discharged from detox at the ____ Center on 7/13/10 and attended an appointment at the ____ on 7/14/10. She was referred to IOP. She reports feeling better and experiencing no withdrawal. She reports a stable mood. She has never had substance abuse treatment prior to this detox. She has been hospitalized three times for treatment for her Bipolar Disorder. She is currently living with her father in an isolated location. Her father's current wife just returned to Canada and they are getting divorced. She reports some stress about that. She also reports that her sister is currently unsupportive maybe due to anger over Liberty's disappearance for the two months when she was injecting meth. She was introduced to injecting through a boyfriend. She has attended 12-Step meetings in the past. She is requesting IOP services voluntarily and meets criteria for admission to IOP.

Note: It was stated prior, "no needle." Question Doc: Are you listening?

Liberty Crouch

~ 104 ~

Entry 9 – Goals Confessed

Name: Crouch, Liberty   SMC LME Client Record

Goals: Abstinence from AOD and to work a good recovery program.

Consumer's Readiness & Motivation to Engage in Treatment: "I have seen the light, I'm tried and my body is tired. I want to be there for my kids."

Assessors' Treatment/Service Recommendations
Recommend SA-IOP and informal supports (12-step meetings, Recovery Education classes such as WRAP), medication evaluation.

Entry 10 – –Action Plan

Problem/Need # 1: Maintain sobriety and work a good recovery program.

Goal A (Measurable) Liberty will attain and maintain abstinence from AOD as evidenced by self report, attendance at recovery meeting, chemical analyses and oservatons of health care providers.	Service: IOP, Recovery Education Center Frequency: 42 IOP group sessions and 10 IOP individual sessions over a 14-week period; 1 social support group per week following completion of IOP.	Responsible Person ...J IOP staff staff	Target Completion Date 7/16/11
Review Date:	Goal Status:	Justification for continuing or discontinuing goal:	

Goal B (Measurable)	Service: Frequency:	Responsible Person	Target Completion Date
Review Date:	Goal Status: Select	Justification for continuing or discontinuing goal:	

Problem/Need # 2: Mood stability and panic disorder.

Liberty will create a wellness management plan which will include developing and implementing effective coping skills, improving mood stability and reducing panic symptoms. She will demonstrate an improved ability to carry out normal responsibilities, improved distress tolerance and regulation of emotions as evidenced by self report, and observations of health care providers.	Service: IOP, Recovery Education Center Frequency: Monitoring symptoms throughout SA-IOP program, with ongoing medication management as necessary.	Responsible Person SA-IOP Clinicians and psychiatric staff prn. REC Staff	Target Completion Date 7/16/11
Review Date:	Goal Status: Select	Justification for continuing or discontinuing goal:	

CONFIDENTIAL AND PRIVILIGED
This information may be protected by Federal Regulation 42 C.F.R. Re-disclosure of this information is prohibited by law without the client/legal representative's written consent. If either should request access to this information they should be referred back to our agency.

Demons Release Trilogies, Book 3

Any Thoughts

Entry 11 - Dr. Sandy Encounter
Date: 08/09/2010

Patient Name: CROUCH, LIBERTY
Provider Name: SANDY
Encounter Date: <None>
Note Date: 08/09/2010

I have explained to the patient the reasons for prescribing the above medication, the expected benefits and the potential side effects. We also discussed the treatment alternatives and the possible risks and benefits of the alternatives, which included the expected course or outcomes without treatment. The patient verbalized understanding and asked appropriate questions.

Counseling and coordination of care 25 minutes

Entry 12 - Note Date: 09/13/2010

Patient Name: CROUCH, LIBERTY
Provider Name:
Encounter Date: <None>
Note Date: 09/13/2010

SA-IOP Discharge Note.....................:
           Time: 18 . 30 , Duration: 0 . 15 , Service Code: Place of Service:

 DISCHARGE SUMMARY/TRANSITION PLAN

Client Name: Liberty Crouch   Client Record No
Date Completed: 9/13/10   Date of last group: 7/30/10

Name and Role of Individual Completing Plan:

Discharge Summary
X Liberty tested positive for Meth on 7/30/10 and denied usage and left the building angry. About a week later she called ready to come back to group. She was told that she would need to meet with us for an individual counseling session prior to coming back. She never came back. She left messages with Sherri several times saying she was in Florida about her breast problems but never came back to group.

Entry 13 – Note Date: 09/21/2010

Patient Name: CROUCH, LIBERTY
Provider Name: SANDY
Encounter Date: <None>
Note Date: 09/21/2010

This information may be protected by Federal Regulation 42 C.F.R. Re-disclosure of this information is prohibited by law without the client/legal representative's written consent. If either should request access to this information they should be referred back to our agency.

Medication Evaluation Progress Note................:
Time: 16.00, Duration: 0.20, Place of Service:

Interim history: Liberty is here today for follow up. She reports that she's "tired all day," and "lacking energy." She states she has to drink multiple energy drinks and takes Sudafed almost daily because of her allergies and cats/dogs at home, which also gives her energy. She says she can't go hiking with her father due to no energy. She wants to come off of her prescription medications and have her father give her herbs instead such as St. John's wort. She says it's her father's idea, "but I'm scared to."

She failed a drug test at SA-IOPT and became very angry by her own account to me and swears she has been clean since July 4th. She believes it was due to the Sudafed she takes almost daily.

She did go to FL because of her "infection" in a blood vessel secondary to "shooting up," and had to have her breast implants replaced. She reports that her face is "breaking out" and wonders if it's from the prescription medication.

She has tolerated the increase of her Abilify to 20mg well, is using the added Vistaril regularly as well as the increased Gabapentin at 400mg tid.

Mental status exam:
Appearance: well groomed, pleasant
Behavior: cooperative
Mood: euthymic
Affect: anxious
Speech: fast rate and volume
Thought process: linear and goal oriented
Thought content: no SI/HI, denies psychosis.
J/I poor to fair
No AIMS

IMPRESSION:
Axis I: Bipolar disorder type I; panic disorder (may be related to substance abuse); PTSD; methamphetamine abuse
Axis II: Borderline personality disorder

PLAN: Liberty is all over the place today in her thinking. She wants to return to SA-IOPT and I fully support that, as this is what she needs most.
1.) I do not recommend stopping her prescription medications and beginning herbs instead. I strongly advise against mixing her prescription medications with herbs and advise her of the dangers of serotonin syndrome.
2.) I advise the discontinuation of Sudafed or pseudoephedrine of any kind due to the side effects of anxiety, insomnia, fluid retention, reduced urination, etc...AND I remind her that it's an ingredient used in the making of methamphetamines.
3.) I don't think her prescription medications have anything to do with her face breaking out. I do advise that it can be related to meth use.
4.) I remind her that this is a process and she needs to remember that she still has a "using" mentality and will use energy drinks, Sudafed or anything else to instantly give her "energy" as that's what she did with meth; however all those things increase her anxiety and panic, so she needs to get off of everything.
5.) In addressing her loss of energy and feeling tired, I refer to #4 above and explain that she will feel tired as she stays clean, and her prescription medicines can make her tired, so the further she gets from using then we can reduce over time her prescription medicine as well (Vistaril, Gabapentin). In the meantime she has to push herself to

Liberty Crouch

Entry 14 – Continued Note Date: 09/21/2010

Patient Name: CROUCH LIBERTY
Provider Name. SANDY
Encounter Date: <None>
Note Date: 09/21/2010

exercise each day whether she feels like it or not.
6.) No medication changes today. She'll remain on Abilify 20mg dailoy, Gabapentin 400mg tid, Trazodone 150mg nightly, and Vistaril 50 to 100 mg up to qid prn for anxiety.
7.) RTC within 2 months for follow up

I have explained to the patient the reasons for prescribing the above medication, the expected benefits and the potential side effects. We also discussed the treatment alternatives and the possible risks and benefits of the alternatives, which included the expected course or outcomes without treatment. The patient verbalized understanding and asked appropriate questions.

Any Thoughts

Demons Release Trilogies, Book 3

Entry 15 – Note Date: 01/03/2011

Patient Name: CROUCH LIBERTY
Provider Name: SANDY
Encounter Date: <None>
Note Date: 01/03/2011

Medication Evaluation Progress Note..............:
Time: 11.00, Duration: 0.25, Service Code   Place of Service

Interim history: Liberty is here today for follow up to discuss her response to medication and her affective symptoms and behaviors. She hasn't begun the herbal treatment as of yet because   so she's waiting until she can afford it or until something changes with   She continues to struggle enormously with anxiety and asks to go back on Xanax or another sedative because "they worked," and she's now 7 months clean. She doesn't think that the Neurotin is helping at all. She says that she's taken as much as 150mg of Vistaril at a time and it "does nothing." She struggles with going out in public. She still doesn't watch TV because it gives her "subliminal messages," and notes it has her whole life. She sees her children every other weekend.

She is now taking pictures with her phone and somehow manipulates the photos, prints them out, frames them and is now selling them. She is also writing a book based on her journal. She calls the pictures, "what do you see?"

Mental status exam:
Appearance: well groomed, pleasant
Behavior: cooperative
Mood: anxious
Affect: anxious
Speech: fast rate, not pressured and normal volume
Thought process: linear and goal oriented
Thought content: no SI/HI, denies psychosis.
J/I poor to fair
No AIMS

IMPRESSION:
Axis I: Bipolar disorder type I; panic disorder (may be related to substance abuse); PTSD; methamphetamine abuse vs dependence (clean x 7 months however she did fail a drug screen at IOPT & never returned)
Axis II: Borderline personality disorder

PLAN: Liberty continues to struggle with anxiety and paranoia. I have strongly recommended that she not mix herbs with her prescription medications.
1. Continue Abilify 20mg daily to target mood symptoms, psychotic features/paranoia
2. Continue Trazodone 150mg po q hs for sleep
3. Taper off of Neurotin and if it wasn't helping for anxiety then stop
4. She's already stopped Vistaril
5. Begin Clonidine 0.2mg, ½ to 1 up to tid prn for her anxiety.
6. RTC in one month for follow up
7. She is willing to begin counseling with Kyler   although states she can't begin for a few weeks due to "weather."

I have explained to the patient the reasons for prescribing the above medication, the expected benefits and the potential side effects. We also discussed the treatment alternatives and the possible risks and benefits of the alternatives, which included the expected course or outcomes without treatment. The patient verbalized understanding and asked appropriate questions.

Liberty Crouch

~ 110 ~

Entry 16 – Note Date: 04/25/2011

Patient Name: CROUCH,
Provider Name: SANDY
Encounter Date: <None>
Note Date: 04/25/2011

Medication Evaluation Progress Note................:
, Time: 13 . 30 , Duration: 0 . 20 , Service Code: , Place of Service

Interim history: Liberty has presented to walk in clinic. She reports that she went off of her medications because her father wanted her to try "herbal remedies" but it didn't work so she restarted her medications. She reports her father has a alcohol problem and he "does stuff at night he doesn't remember in the morning." She states he held a gun to her and her boyfriend one time. He "kicked me out and I wasn't ready to leave." She's reports she's been "picking at her face," has covered her mirrors and struggles with going out in public. She still doesn't watch TV because it gives her "subliminal messages," and notes it has her whole life. She thinks the world is going to end in May. She reports increased depression and doesn't think her medications are working. She denies any relapses with drugs. She can fall asleep with the Trazodone but wakes up prematurely.

Mental status exam:
Appearance: no make-up, sores on her face, very thin
Behavior: cooperative
Mood: anxious
Affect; blunted
Speech: fast rate, not pressured and normal volume
Thought process: linear and goal oriented
Thought content: no SI/HI, ideas of reference, thought insertion, paranoia
J/I poor to fair
No AIMS

PROPERTY OF
~VICES
CONFIDENTIAL AND PRIVILIGED
This information may be protected by Federal Regulation 42 C.F.R. Re-disclosure of this information is prohibited by law without the client/legal representative's written consent. If either should request access to this information they should be referred back to our agency.

IMPRESSION:
Axis I: Bipolar disorder type I; panic disorder (may be related to substance abuse); PTSD; methamphetamine dependence
Axis II: Borderline personality disorder

PLAN: Liberty has increased depression and psychotic features. She says she's not using however it appears that she may be.—
1. Increase Abilify to 30mg daily to target mood symptoms, psychotic features/paranoia
2. Increase Trazodone to 200mg po q hs for sleep
5. Continue Clonidine 0.2mg, ½ to 1 up to tid prn for her anxiety.
6. RTC in one month for follow up and come to walk-in clinic in two weeks for follow up as well.

| Judgement |

I have explained to the patient the reasons for prescribing the above medication, the expected benefits and the potential side effects. We also discussed the treatment alternatives and the possible risks and benefits of the alternatives, which included the expected course or outcomes without treatment. The patient verbalized understanding and asked appropriate questions.

Demons Release Trilogies, Book 3

Entry 17 - Note Date: 06/02/2011

Patient Name: CROUCH, LIBERTY
Provider Name: . , , SANDY
Encounter Date: <None>
Note Date: 06/02/2011

PROPERTY OF
CONFIDENTIAL AND PRIVILEGED ES
This information may be protected by Federal Regulation 42 C.F.R. Re-disclosure of this information is prohibited by law without the client/legal representative's written consent. If either should request access to this information they should be referred back to our agency.

Medication Evaluation Progress Note..............:
I , Time: 14 . 20 , Duration: 0 . 20 , Service Code , Place of Service

Interim history: Liberty has presented to walk in clinic. She reports that the Trazodone at the higher dose of 200mg isn't working well for sleep. It makes her groggy in the morning and if she doesn't fall asleep during the "15 minute window" she's up for hours and feeling strange. She also began the Neurotin again but only takes it twice daily.

Mental status exam:
Appearance: groomed, looks like she's in better condition than when I saw her last
Behavior: cooperative
Mood: anxious
Affect: broader range today
Speech: normal rate and tone
Thought process: linear and goal oriented
Thought content: no SI/HI, no psychotic features or paranoia detected or expressed today
J/I fair
No AIMS

IMPRESSION:
Axis I: Bipolar disorder type I; panic disorder (may be related to substance abuse); PTSD; methamphetamine dependence
Axis II: Borderline personality disorder

PLAN: Liberty appears to be doing better and her mood is more stable although she continues to struggle with sleep and also tells me that she's congested in her sinus area.
1. Continue Abilify to 30mg daily to target mood symptoms, psychotic features/paranoia
2. Begin Ambien 10mg po q hs prn for insomnia and may add Trazodone 50mg to it if needed.
5. Continue Clonidine 0.2mg, ½ to 1 up to tid prn for her anxiety.
6. Continue Neurotin 400mg po bid to target mood and anxiety
6. May use Claritin D for sinus issues.
6. RTC in one month for follow up

I have explained to the patient the reasons for prescribing the above medication, the expected benefits and the potential side effects. We also discussed the treatment alternatives and the possible risks and benefits of the alternatives, which included the expected course or outcomes without treatment. The patient verbalized understanding and asked appropriate questions.

Entry 18 – Note Date: 10/04/2011

Patient Name: CROUCH, LIBERTY
Provider Name: ANDY   PROPERTY OF
Encounter Date: <None>   CONFIDENTIAL AND PRIVILEGED ...RVICES
Note Date: 10/04/2011

This information may be protected by Federal Regulation 42 C.F.R. Re-disclosure of this information is prohibited by law without the client/legal representative's written consent. If either should request access to this information they should be referred back to our agency.

Medication Evaluation Progress Note.............:
RU: 326, Time: 15:00, Duration: 0:20, Service Code: 90862, Place of Service: 11

Interim history: Liberty is here today to discuss her response to medications and her affective symptoms and behaviors. She continues to struggle with anxiety and some mood issues. She says she clean and sober. She continues to have odd beliefs and be somewhat paranoid.   **[Odd to who, Doc?]**

Mental status exam:
Appearance: groomed, cooperative
Behavior: cooperative
Mood: anxious
Affect: anxious
Speech: normal rate and tone
Thought process: linear and goal oriented
Thought content: no SI/HI, no psychotic features or paranoia detected or expressed today   **[Contradictory: Which is it, Doc? Paranoia or not. Just saying.]**
J/I   fair/fair
No AIMS

IMPRESSION:
Axis I: Bipolar disorder type I; panic disorder (may be related to substance abuse); PTSD; methamphetamine dependence
Axis II: Borderline personality disorder

PLAN: Liberty appears to be at her baseline.
1. Continue Abilify to 30mg daily to target mood symptoms, psychotic features/paranoia
2. Continue Ambien 10mg po q hs prn for insomnia and may add Trazodone 50mg to it if needed.
5. Continue Clonidine 0.2mg, ½ to 1 up to tid prn for her anxiety.
6. Continue Neurotin 400mg po bid to target mood and anxiety
7. RTC in within 3 months for follow up

I have explained to the patient the reasons for prescribing the above medication, the expected benefits and the potential side effects. We also discussed the treatment alternatives and the possible risks and benefits of the alternatives, which included the expected course or outcomes without treatment. The patient verbalized understanding and asked appropriate questions.

Any Thoughts

Entry 19 – Note Date: 11/10/2011

Patient Name: CROUCH LIBERTY
Provider Name: , SANDY
Encounter Date: <None>
Note Date: 11/10/2011

CONFIDENTIAL AND PRIVILEGED -ES
This information may be protected by Federal Regulation 42 C.F.R. Re-disclosure of this information is prohibited by law without the client/legal representative's written consent. If either should request access to this information they should be referred back to our agency.

Medication Evaluation Progress Note...............:
RI   Time: 13.30, Duration: 0.20, Service Code: , Place of Service.

Interim history: Liberty is here today to discuss her response to medications and her affective symptoms and behaviors. She continues to struggle with anxiety and some mood issues. The Buspar hasn't helped and she's having difficulty tolerating it. She is now in her own apartment and doesn't want to give up her cat, "Kitty" because she's so comforting to her and she is now on her own. Liberty mentions that when she was a teen she was on Lithium and it seemed to help. She continues to have hypomania, cleans obsessively and racing thoughts. She's been clean now for over a year.

Mental status exam:
Appearance: groomed, cooperative
Behavior: cooperative
Mood: anxious
Affect: anxious
Speech: normal rate and tone
Thought process: linear and goal oriented
Thought content: no SI/HI, no hallucinations, some paranoia
J/I fair/fair
No AIMS
Weight 121
Height 5'1"
BP 142/80
HR 60

IMPRESSION:
Axis I: Bipolar disorder type I; panic disorder (may be related to substance abuse); PTSD; methamphetamine dependence
Axis II: Borderline personality disorder

PLAN: Liberty continues to struggle with anxiety, hypomania and is afraid of losing her cat.
1.   Continue Abilify to 30mg daily to target mood symptoms, psychotic features/paranoia
2.   Continue Ambien 10mg po q hs prn for insomnia and may add Trazodone 50mg to it if needed.
5.   Continue Clonidine 0.2mg, ½ to 1 up to tid prn for her anxiety.
6.   Begin Eskalith CR 450mg 1 po daily x7 days then 1 po bid as a mood stabilizer to target symptoms of mania and racing thoughts. After 2 weeks she'll obtain labs, lithium level, cr, and TSH
7.   Stop Buspar as its ineffective and she's having side effects
7.   RTC in within 3 weeks for follow up

I have explained to the patient the reasons for prescribing the above medication, the expected benefits and the potential side effects. We also discussed the treatment alternatives and the possible risks and benefits of the alternatives, which included the expected course or outcomes without treatment. The patient verbalized understanding and asked appropriate questions.

Liberty Crouch

Entry 20 – Mediation Management
Date: 02/06/2012

Session Information

Client:	Crouch, Liberty
Staff:	Sandy
Service Date/Time:	2/6/2012 1:00 PM - 1:23 PM
Client Program:	Medical Psychiatric Services (MED)
Activity:	Med Check / Psychiatric Followup (MED)
Organization:	
Service Location:	

Goal(s) Addressed

No Goal(s) addressed were chosen

Goal(s) Addressed: medication management

Psychiatric Medical Followup Note v2b

Interval History / Subjective: Liberty is here today to discuss her response to medications and her affective symptoms and behaviors. She says she's an "emotional wreck." She had tried to call me but when I called her she hadn't set up her voice mail and I couldn't get through. She was off her medications because she ran out for a week and now has been on them for 2 days. She is depressed "I can't get out of the bed, but I'm not sleeping at night." she reports daily panic attacks.

Primary Care Provider: Dr.

Care Coordination with PCP? ○ Yes ● No

Tobacco Use: ● Current Use ○ In Remission ○ Never Used

Objective:
Appearance: groomed, cooperative
Behavior: cooperative
Mood: anxious
Affect: tearful
Speech: fastl rate and normal tone
Thought process: linear and goal oriented
Thought content: no SI/HI, no hallucinations, some paranoia
J/I fair/fair
No AIMS

Discussion / Plans: Liberty ran out of her medications and was called in 10mg of Abilify instead of 30. She reports depression and panic attacks
1. Increase back to Abilify to 30mg daily to target mood symptoms, psychotic features/paranoia
2. Continue Ambien 10mg po q hs prn for insomnia and may add Trazodone 100mg to it if needed
5. Continue Clonidine 0.2mg, to 1 up to tid prn for her anxiety
6. Continue Eskalith CR 450mg 1 po bid for moods stability and when she returns lab work will be needed
7. Begin Remeron 15mg nightly to target symptoms of depression and help with sleep. She may be able to use this alone and stop Ambien and Trazodone.
7. RTC in within 2 months for follow up as transportation is difficult for her. She'll call if she has any problems in the meantime or if symptoms don't improve

I have explained to the patient the reasons for prescribing the above medication, the expected benefits and the potential side effects. We also discussed the treatment alternatives and the possible risks and benefits of the alternatives, which included the expected course or outcomes without treatment. The patient verbalized understanding and asked appropriate questions.

Entry 21 – Note Date: 02/06/2012
No Mediations Found

2/6/2012   Liberty Crouch

Client Medications

Begin Date	End Date	Amount/Refills	Status
No Client Medications found			

Vitals Entry

Date:	02/06/2012 01:27 PM
Blood Pressure:	0
Heart Rate:	
Respiration Rate:	
Temperature:	Fahrenheit
Height:	Inches 61.5
Weight:	Pounds 121
BMI:	22.49
Pain Scale:	

Client DSM Diagnosis as of 2/6/2012

Client:	Crouch, Liberty
Date Diagnosed:	2/6/2012
Diagnosis By:	Sandy
External Diagnosis?	No
Description:	

Diagnostic Formulation

Axis I: Clinical Disorders

DSM Code - Description	ICD-9 Code - Short Description	Pri/Sec	Comments
295.70 - Schizoaffective Disorder	295.72 - SCHIZOAFFECTIVE DIS-CHR	1	Bipolar Type
304.20 - Cocaine Dependence	304.20 - COCAINE DEPEND-UNSPEC	2	in partial remission
304.40 - Amphetamine Dependence	304.40 - AMPHETAMIN DEPEND-UNSPEC	2	in partial remission

Axis II: Personality Disorders and Mental Retardation

DSM Code - Description	ICD-9 Code - Short Description	Pri/Sec	Comments
V71.09 - No Diagnosis on Axis II	V71.09 - OBSERV-MENTAL COND NEC		

Axis III: General Medical Conditions

Liberty Crouch

Entry 22 – Continued Note Date: 02/06/2012

2/6/2012   Liberty   Crouch

Description	Pri/Sec
No Medical Problems Noted	

Axis IV: Psychosocial and Environmental Problems

Description	Severity	Comments
No Psychosocial or Environmental Problems Noted		

Axis V: Global Assessment of Functioning Scale

Current GAF Score	39

Signatures

Signature #1: | Sandy   6/2012 2:02 PM

Signature History

Action	Date	Staff
Document Signed	2/6/2012	Sandy

Any Thoughts

Demons Release Trilogies, Book 3

Entry 23 – Note Date: 05/21/2012
Problem Depression

Session Information

Client:	Crouch, Liberty
Staff:	Don
Service Date/Time:	5/21/2012 1:40 PM - 2:20 PM
Client Program:	Medical Psychiatric Services (MED)
Activity:	Med Check / Psychiatric Followup (MED)
Organization:	
Service Location:	- Office

Goal(s) Addressed

REC Treatment Plan

Problem Depression
Goal To receive medication management and medication evaluation

Goal(s) Addressed:

Psychiatric Medical Followup Note v2b

Interval History / Subjective: Liberty is here today for a recheck. She feels that her depression is not as severe but she continues to have a lot of variation in her moods. Some days she will be depressed and other days she will feel much better and it sounds as though she may be almost hypomanic on some days.

She does continue on lithium 450 mg twice a day, Ambien 10 mg daily at bedtime, trazodone 100 mg daily at bedtime, Abilify 30 mg daily at bedtime, clonidine 0.2 mg 3 times a day.

She also tells me that she is having frequent migraine headaches. These occur about every other day. She is on Imitrex which helps somewhat.

> There was information here I am not sharing for privacy. It mentioned another patient at the same facility.

Primary Care Provider: Dr
Care Coordination with PCP? ○ Yes ● No
Tobacco Use: ● Current Use ○ In Remission ○ Never Used
Objective: Appearance: groomed, cooperative
Behavior: cooperative
Mood: Slightly depressed
Affect: Restricted
Speech: Normal rate and normal tone
Thought process: linear and goal oriented
Thought content: no SI/HI, no hallucinations, some paranoia
J/I fair/fair
No AIMS

Discussion / Plans: 1. Schizoaffective disorder, bipolar type. This is somewhat better but can still be significantly improved. I will let Topamax. We will start at 25 mg daily and taper up to 50 mg twice a day and 4 weeks. She will follow up at that time. Continue lithium, Abilify, trazodone. Consider getting a lithium level at the next visit and increasing the dose if possible.

2. Frequent migraine headaches. The Topamax may help this as well. She is to followup with Dr. regarding this.

Entry 24 – Continued Note Date: 05/21/2012

Client Medications

Begin Date	End Date	Amount/Refills	Status
No Client Medications found.			

Vitals Entry

Date:	05/21/2012 01:42 PM
Blood Pressure:	144 88
Heart Rate:	64
Respiration Rate:	
Temperature:	Fahrenheit
Height:	Inches 62
Weight:	Pounds 124.4
BMI:	22.75
Pain Scale:	

Client DSM Diagnosis as of 5/21/2012

Client:	Crouch, Liberty
Date Diagnosed:	5/21/2012
Diagnosis By:	Don [
External Diagnosis?	No
Description:	

Diagnostic Formulation

Axis I: Clinical Disorders

DSM Code - Description	ICD-9 Code - Short Description	Pri/Sec	Comments
295.70 - Schizoaffective Disorder	295.72 - SCHIZOAFFECTIVE DIS-CHR	1	Bipolar Type;
304.20 - Cocaine Dependence	304.20 - COCAINE DEPEND-UNSPEC	2	in partial remission
304.40 - Amphetamine Dependence	304.40 - AMPHETAMIN DEPEND-UNSPEC	2	in partial remission

Axis II: Personality Disorders and Mental Retardation

DSM Code - Description	ICD-9 Code - Short Description	Pri/Sec	Comments
V71.09 - No Diagnosis on Axis II	V71.09 - OBSERV-MENTAL COND NEC		

Axis III: General Medical Conditions

Demons Release Trilogies, Book 3

Entry 25 – Note Date: 08/17/2012

Session Information

Client: Crouch, Liberty
Staff: Scott (
Service Date/Time: 8/17/2012 11:30 AM - 12:00 PM

Client Program: Medical Psychiatric Services (MED)
Activity: Med Check / Psychiatric Followup (MED)

Organization:
Service Location: - Office

Goal(s) Addressed

No Goal(s) addressed were chosen

Goal(s) Addressed: compliance and a decrease of symptoms

Psychiatric Medical Followup Note v2b

Interval History / Subjective:
Name: Liberty Crouch
DOB:
DOS: 8/17/12

DIAGNOSIS: Schizoaffective; Cocaine Dep; Amphet Dep

MEDICATIONS: Lithium 450mg bid; Ambien 10mg; Trazodone 100mg; Abilify 30mg Clonidine 0.2mg TID; Topamax 50mg

SUBJECTIVE:
-Reports that she has seen Dr.   recently and was taken off lithium, ambien, Topamax and transitioned to VPA
-Now taking VPA, trazodone, stool softener and clonidine
-Felt that she has been in bed for a week; feels withdrawing from medications
-Currently taking 4 tabs per day; started on the 9th
-Felt that the VPA would be replacement for other meds
-Limited functional abilities
-Mood has been "blah"
-Felt that she was doing fine other than paranoid with the addition of Topamax
-Topamax was helpful for the migraines but made her "delusional and paranoid"
-Denies SI/HI

Primary Care Provider: Dr. .
Care Coordination with PCP? ○ Yes ● No
Tobacco Use: ● Current Use   ○ In Remission   ○ Never Used

Objective:
OBJECTIVE:
Mental Status Exam:
Appearance: Mildly disheveled; casually dressed; and pale skin and a sickly looking
Cooperation: Good
Eye Contact: Good
Psychomotor: Mildly agitated.
Speech: Mildly elevated rate
Mood: Dysphoric
Affect: Congruent with stated mood
Thought Processes: Linear and logical
Thought Content: No SI/HI; no notable perceptual disturbance
Insight: Poor to fair
Judgment: Fair
Cognition: Alert and oriented X4

Liberty Crouch

Entry 26 – Continued Note Date: 08/17/2012

Side Effects: None

Labs: None to report

Suicide Risk Assessment: No SI/HI, felt to be appropriate for outpt care at this time. Protective factors include duty to self, family and ongoing desire for treatment and symptom relief. Currently felt to be at low/baseline risk of harm to self or others.

Discussion / Plans:
ASSESSMENT/PLAN:
-AXIS I: Schizoaffective disorder. Cocaine and methamphetamine dependence.
-AXIS II: Deferred
-AXIS III: Migraine headaches
-AXIS IV:
-AXIS V: GAF:

-Patient presents today for medication management followup; it should be noted that she was 20 min. late for her appointment. The patient indicates that she has not been feeling well since her primary care physician apparently took her off of number of different medications. She states that he discontinued her lithium, Abilify, Topamax and placed her on Depakote of an unknown dosage. Since then she has felt ill and increase in substantial migraine pain and associated limited functionality.

-Restart Topamax 50 mg one half tab by mouth daily at bedtime x3 days then one half tab by mouth twice a day, then 1 tab in the morning and one half at night and finally 50 mg twice a day after roughly a weeks titration. She indicates that this medication causes "delusions" but with further discuss. She is copacetic with this order to take care of her migraines.

-May attempt to contact her primary care physician in order to elucidate why he transitioned patient from so many medications when previous notes indicate that she is doing fine on the combination. I can look to reinstate her previous medications as necessary.

-Reiterated an attempt to discover why she didn't transitioned to another medication however she was uncertain why this was. Patient appeared in considerable distress, given her subjective feelings and was headed back home to go to bed.

-Informed Consent: Discussion was had regarding medication information including classification, indication for use, dose and route of administration. Discussed risks, side effects, benefits and multiple alternative forms of psychopharmacologic medications (including risk of not having treatment). Patient was an active participant in developing treatment plan including use of psychopharmacologic medications and had the opportunity to ask questions (with answers provided to patient's approval). Patient verbalized understanding of the information provided and is in agreement with plan. Patient is felt to have capacity at this time to make decisions regarding treatment and able to give informed consent/voice a voluntary choice for treatment.

-Psychopathology of identified problem explained; psychoeducation provided.

-Encouraged patient to use all available treatment modalities offered including, for example, relaxation techniques, therapy and medication use as described above.

-Directed patient to live healthy lifestyle including, but not limited to, proper diet and exercise (to the extent of their physical abilities/capabilities/limitations).

-RTC 1 mo, sooner if nec.

Client Medications

Begin Date	End Date	Amount/Refills	Status
No Client Medications found.			

Entry 27 – Continued Note Date: 08/17/2012

Vitals Entry

Date:	08/18/2012 12:01 AM
Blood Pressure:	
Heart Rate:	
Respiration Rate:	
Temperature:	Fahrenheit
Height:	Inches 62
Weight:	Pounds 124.4
BMI:	22.75
Pain Scale:	

Client DSM Diagnosis as of 8/17/2012

Client:	Crouch, Liberty
Date Diagnosed:	8/17/2012
Diagnosis By:	Scott ( )
External Diagnosis?	No
Description:	

Diagnostic Formulation

Axis I: Clinical Disorders

DSM Code - Description	ICD-9 Code - Short Description	Pri/Sec	Comments
295.70 - Schizoaffective Disorder	295.72 - SCHIZOAFFECTIVE DIS-CHR	1	Bipolar Type
304.20 - Cocaine Dependence	304.20 - COCAINE DEPEND-UNSPEC	2	in partial remission
304.40 - Amphetamine Dependence	304.40 - AMPHETAMIN DEPEND-UNSPEC	2	in partial remission

Axis II: Personality Disorders and Mental Retardation

DSM Code - Description	ICD-9 Code - Short Description	Pri/Sec	Comments
V71.09 - No Diagnosis on Axis II	V71.09 - OBSERV-MENTAL COND NEC		

Axis III: General Medical Conditions

Description	Pri/Sec
Migraine Headaches	2

Axis IV: Psychosocial and Environmental Problems

Liberty Crouch

Liberty Crouch

Any Thoughts

Entry 28 – Note Date: 12/31/2012
Medication Management & Evaluation

12/31/2012 Liberty Crouch

Session Information

Client:	Crouch, Liberty (
Staff:	Scott (
Service Date/Time:	12/31/2012 1:40 PM - 2:00 PM
Client Program:	
Activity:	Med Check / Psychiatric Followup (MED)
Organization:	
Service Location:	- Office

Goal(s) Addressed

REC Treatment Plan

	Problem	Depression
☒	Goal	To receive medication management and medication evaluation

Goal(s) Addressed:

Psychiatric Medical Followup Note v2b

Interval History / Subjective:

Name: Liberty Crouch

DIAGNOSIS: Schizoaffective; Cocaine Dep; Amphet Dep

MEDICATIONS: Lithium 450mg bid; Ambien 10mg; Trazodone 100mg; Abilify 30mg Clonidine 0.2mg TID, Topamax 50mg

SUBJECTIVE:
- Pt reports that has been traveling
- Pt has been off medications; currently taking trazodone, clonidine, Topamax
- "I need something for bipolar"
- Went off of lithium and abilify because "I don't like it"
- Pt reports being paranoid; feels that someone may be coming to get her every night; has weapons; feels relieved in the mornings when it does not happen
- Pt reports being goal directed; "obsessively in the mirror"; changing outfits;
- Last time used cocaine and meth about 3-5yrs ago, respectively
- Feels constipation with clonidine
- Past h/o Xanax and klonopin helpful for anxiety; feels that she is having multiple panic attacks throughout the week as well as ongoing anxiety
- Now feels that the Topamax has been helpful and not causing delusional thoughts

Primary Care Provider:
Care Coordination with PCP? ○ Yes ○ No

Tobacco Use: ● Current Use   ○ In Remission   ○ Never Used

Objective: Mental Status Exam:
Appearance: casually dressed
Cooperation: Good initially but became extremely upset and notable frustrated when not provided Xanax or klonopin scripts
Attitude: sarcastic and inflamatory
Eye Contact: Intense
Psychomotor: agitated
Speech: Mildly elevated rate
Mood: Dysphoric

Entry 29 – Continued Note Date: 12/31/2012

Affect: Congruent with stated mood and angry
Thought Processes: Linear and logical
Thought Content: No SI/HI; no notable perceptual disturbance
Insight: Poor
Judgment: Poor
Cognition: Alert and oriented X4

Side Effects: constipation

Labs: None to report

Suicide Risk Assessment: No SI/HI; felt to be appropriate for outpt care at this time. Protective factors include duty to self, family and ongoing desire for treatment and symptom relief. Currently felt to be at low/baseline risk of harm to self or others.

ASSESSMENT/PLAN:
-AXIS I: Schizoaffective disorder. Cocaine and methamphetamine dependence
-AXIS II: Deferred
-AXIS III: Migraine headaches
-AXIS IV: housing
-AXIS V: GAF: 51

Discussion / Plans: -Patient presents today for medication management followup; last seen 4 mo ago. She has been apparently without medications for some months; has been dealing with increased anxiety and thoughts of possibly being attacked at night. Likely that her paranoia and possible decompensation without meds has led to her elevated anxiety. Pt became extremely upset when discussing her past use of Xanax and klonopin and not feeling that they would be appropriate given previous h/o meth and cocaine dependence. She seemed to interpret my explanation as pejorative despite my reasoning that providing a potentially addictive substance was not appropriate

-Restart Abilify 15mg: x1wk then 1x1wk then 2 thereafter to get her back to 30mg she was previously taking
-Continue Topamax for headaches
-Start vistaril 50mg tid prn anxiety
-Suggest d/c of clonidine given side effects and limited subjective benefit
-D/C lithium, ambien as she is no longer taking these

-Provided option to see a different provider if she was not comfortable with the decision to defer bzds but she indicated that she will f/u

-Informed Consent: Discussion was had regarding medication information including classification, indication for use, dose and route of administration. Discussed risks, side effects, benefits and multiple alternative forms of psychopharmacologic medications (including risk of not having treatment). Patient was an active participant in developing treatment plan including use of psychopharmacologic medications and had the opportunity to ask questions (with answers provided to patient's approval). Patient verbalized understanding of the information provided and is in agreement with plan. Patient is felt to have capacity at this time to make decisions regarding treatment and able to give informed consent/voice a voluntary choice for treatment

-Psychopathology of identified problem explained; psychoeducation provided.

-Encouraged patient to use all available treatment modalities offered including, for example, relaxation techniques, therapy and medication use as described above.

-Directed patient to live healthy lifestyle including, but not limited to, proper diet and exercise (to the extent of their physical abilities/capabilities/limitations).

-RTC 2 mo, sooner if nec. Pt understanding of crisis line and supportive staff

Client Medications

Entry 30 – Diagnosis as of 12/31/2012

12/31/2012   Liberty Crouch

Begin Date	End Date	Amount/Refills	Status
8/27/2012	(Not Set)	30/3	Active

Medication and Dosage: Topamax (topiramate) 100 mg tablet 1/2 tablet
Sig: Take 1/2 tablet by mouth twice a day

Vitals Entry

Date:	12/31/2012 02:19 PM
Blood Pressure:	130 / 90
Heart Rate:	
Respiration Rate:	
Temperature:	Fahrenheit
Height:	Inches 62
Weight:	Pounds 116
BMI:	21.21
Pain Scale:	

Client DSM Diagnosis as of 12/31/2012

Client:	Crouch, Liberty
Date Diagnosed:	12/31/2012
Diagnosis By:	Scott
External Diagnosis?	No
Description:	

Diagnostic Formulation

Axis I: Clinical Disorders

DSM Code - Description	ICD-9 Code - Short Description	Pri/Sec	Comments
295.70 - Schizoaffective Disorder	295.72 - SCHIZOAFFECTIVE DIS-CHR	1	Bipolar Type;
304.20 - Cocaine Dependence	304.20 - COCAINE DEPEND-UNSPEC	2	in partial remission
304.40 - Amphetamine Dependence	304.40 - AMPHETAMIN DEPEND-UNSPEC	2	in partial remission

Axis II: Personality Disorders and Mental Retardation

DSM Code - Description	ICD-9 Code - Short Description	Pri/Sec	Comments
V71.09 - No Diagnosis on Axis II	V71.09 - OBSERV-MENTAL COND NEC		

Description	Pri/Sec

Liberty Crouch

Entry 31 – Note Date: 01/23/2013
Problem Depression

Session Information

Client:	Crouch, Liberty (
Staff:	Katie (
Service Date/Time:	1/23/2013 8:20 AM - 8:30 AM
Client Program:	
Activity:	Individual Therapy (IND)
Organization:	
Service Location:	Office

Goal(s) Addressed

REC Treatment Plan

Problem Depression
Goal To receive medication management and medication evaluation

Goal(s) Addressed:

REC Progress Note

INTERVENTION SECTION

Intervention: Issues/Symptoms/Challenges Processed: Recovery Skills/Tools/Techniques Taught

Provided support, encouragement, and remined Liberty it was her choice to choose to meet with the doctor. Identified common expeirences others have shared when triggered.

Was a formal Risk Assessment done as part of this intervention?
○ Yes
● No

OUTCOME SECTION

Outcome: How did the individual respond to the intervention named above? How is the individual progressing towards goals? What is the plan from here?
Met with Liberty after she walked into the exam room and became triggered.

Student Status: Additional Learning About The Student: What did you learn about the student that others may need to know?

Signatures

Signature #1: Katie — 1/24/2013 10:00 PM

Signature History

Action	Date	Staff
Document Signed	1/24/2013	Katie

Demons Release Trilogies, Book 3

Entry 32 – Continued Note Date: 01/23/2013

Date:	01/23/2013
	08:32 AM
Blood Pressure:	118
	80
Heart Rate:	
Respiration Rate:	
Temperature:	Fahrenheit
Height:	Inches
	61.5
Weight:	Pounds
	118.4
BMI:	22.01
Pain Scale:	

CLIENT COPY

Additional Services

Setting:	○ Inpatient
	● Outpatient
Client Status:	○ New Patient ● Existing Patient ○ Consultation
Was >50% of time used for counseling:	○ Yes
	● No
Total Psychotherapy time (minutes):	

Evaluation and Management Calculator

History Type	Exam Type	MDM Type
○ None	○ None	○ None
○ Problem Focused	○ Problem Focused	○ Straightforward
○ Expanded Problem Focused	○ Expanded Problem Focused	○ Low Complexity
● Detailed	● Detailed	● Moderate Complexity
○ Comprehensive	○ Comprehensive	○ High Complexity

E/M Level: 4

Signatures

Signature #1: Don   ) - 1/23/2013 12:38 PM

Signature History

Action	Date	Staff
Document Signed	1/23/2013	Don

Liberty Crouch

Any Thoughts

Entry 33 – The Battle of the Mind

Session Information

Client: Crouch, Liberty
Staff: Don
Service Date/Time: 1/23/2013 8:30 AM - 9:30 AM

Client Program:
Activity: (Medical)
Organization:
Service Location: Office

Medical Template

HPI: Liberty is here today for an integrated care medical visit. She has schizoaffective disorder. She currently is only taking trazodone 100 mg daily at bedtime, clonidine 0.2 mg 3 times a day, and Topamax. Topamax is primarily for her migraine headaches and she is not sure of the dose of this. She has been prescribed some mood stabilizers and atypical antipsychotics but she does not take these because she is afraid of weight gain or side effects. She has been reading about Invega and is willing to try this.

She has a lot of paranoia that somebody is going to break in and harm her. She has difficulty sleeping because of this. She does not like to leave her house. She has a driver's license but does not have a vehicle. Her brother brings her today.

She is asking for some type of radiologic procedure to diagnose her mental illness.

Review of Systems: Denies any history of heart disease, chest pain, palpitations, edema. She reports a h/o HTN. Denies any dysuria or urinary frequency. Denies any diarrhea or rectal bleeding. She does have constipation. She does not take anything for this. Denies a history of hepatitis, cancer, or blood clots. She has had intermittent dizziness. Denies any numbness. Denies any cough or shortness of breath. Denies any double or blurred vision. Denies any recent weight gain or weight loss. Menses occur about twice a week. She is not sexually active.

PMHx: History of a thyroid abnormality 2 years ago that was never followed up on. She had some preliminary lab work showed a decreased TSH and a decreased free T4.
She has had 2 children. They both live with their father.

PSHx / PFHx: She lives alone. Her brother will help transport her. He lives nearby. She does smoke but is trying to stop.

Strong family history of multiple family members having significant mental illness.

Objective: Blood pressure is 118. Pulse is 70 and regular. Weight is 118 pounds. Neck without thyromegaly or lymphadenopathy. Lungs sounds are clear bilaterally. Heart is regular rate and rhythm without murmur. Abdomen is soft and nontender. No organomegaly or masses. There is no distention or stool felt. Ankles without edema. DTRs are 2+ and equal in both knees. Gait is normal. She is calm and conversant today.

Data Reviewed: I did review some lab work from 2 years ago that showed a decreased TSH, decreased free T4, borderline-low hemoglobin and a borderline-low potassium.

Assessment / Plan: 1. Schizoaffective disorder. I will start her on Invega 3 mg daily. She was given samples and will let us know how this goes. Follow up with me or .
Continue counseling

2. History of hyperthyroidism. We'll recheck thyroid function tests.

3. Health maintenance. She is trying to get in to ▬▬▬ to get a GYN exam and Pap smear. She has also seen Sally ▬▬▬ in the past.

Tests Ordered: She will go to the hospital and have labs drawn. I have asked them to do a TSH, free T4, free T3, comprehensive panel, CBC.

Vitals Entry

Liberty Crouch

Entry 34 – Note Date: 01/28/2013

Session Information

Client: Crouch, Liberty
Staff: Katie
Service Date/Time: 1/28/2013 8:30 AM - 8:40 AM

Client Program:
Activity: Individual Therapy (IND)
Organization:
Service Location: Office

Goal(s) Addressed

REC Treatment Plan

Problem: Depression
Goal: To receive medication management and medication evaluation

Goal(s) Addressed:

REC Progress Note

INTERVENTION SECTION

Intervention: Issues/Symptoms/Challenges Processed; Recovery Skills/Tools/Techniques Taught
Touched base with Libety to see how medication consistency was going and whether she was able to connect with an individual therapy appointment. Provided feedback about ways Liberty was taking care of herself and allowing others to give input. Discussed the option of completing seekign safety and explained the concept.

Was a formal Risk Assessment done as part of this intervention?
○ Yes
● No

OUTCOME SECTION

Outcome: How did the individual respond to the intervention named above? How is the individual progressing towards goals? What is the plan from here?
Liberty plans to connect with ▓▓ about Trazadone she is out of. She reports she felt less hypervigilence at night and is hoping it will continue. liberty will attend an apointment with Lynne ▓▓▓ this week.

Student Status:
Additional Learning About The Student: What did you learn about the student that others may need to know?

Signatures

Signature #1: Katie — 1/29/2013 11:46 PM

Signature History

Action	Date	Staff

Demons Release Trilogies, Book 3

Entry 35 - Next Up the Psychologist
Date: 02/04/2013

PERSONAL CHECKLIST

Name: Lynne Crouch
Date: 2-4-13

Please check all of the following that apply to you now. Put a double check by those that you would like to address in therapy.

- ✓ Feel isolated
- Suicidal thoughts
- ✓ Fatigue
- ✓ Weight changes
- ✓ Eating disorder
- ✓ Changes in sleep
- Difficulty concentrating
- ✓ Trouble remembering
- ✓ Low self-esteem
- ✓ Unsatisfactory relationships
- Trouble dating
- ✓ Unable to make friends *judging in ways*
- Inferiority feelings
- Family concerns
- Sexual orientation
- Alcohol use
- Other drug use
- Academic difficulty
- Home conditions
- ✓ Unusual experiences
- ✓ Highly suspicious of others
- Dizziness
- ✓ Stomach trouble
- Trouble breathing
- Sexual issues
- Cultural issues
- Physical Abuse
- ✓ ACOA (Adult Children of Alcoholic(s))
- ✓ Adjustment to disability
- ✓ Unusual thoughts

- ✓ Depressed
- ✓ Crying spells
- ✓ Appetite change
- ✓ Feel panic
- ✓ Feel tense
- ✓ Unable to relax
- Difficulty studying
- ✓ Loss of enjoyment
- Angry
- ✓ Issues of trust ✓
- ✓ Assertiveness
- Shy
- ✓ Anxiety
- ✓ Loss or grief issues
- ✓ Sexual Abuse — *past issue*
- Trouble with the law
- ✓ Financial difficulty
- ✓ Decision-making
- ✓ Employment difficulty
- ✓ Overly sensitive
- ✓ Unusual behaviors
- ✓ Headaches
- ✓ Fainting spells
- Palpitations
- Want to hurt others
- Rape/Sexual assault
- ✓✓ Relationship/marital difficulty ✓
- ✓ Adjustment to chronic illness
- Self-mutilating
- Destructive

Other: please specify I need to not not get _____ we have alot of ____ _____ only a ____ issues today I get overwhelmed easy ok. thanks :)

Lynne
ptq1

Entry 36 – Initial Contact Report from the Psychologist
Date: 02/04/2013

Initial Contact Report

Date of Contact: February 4, 2013
Client: Liberty Crouch   Therapist: Lynne

Demographic/Diversity Information: Liberty is a 33-year-old Caucasian female. She has 3 children who live in FL with their father.

Summary of Therapy and Recommendations:
- She stated that she is troubled by picking her skin. She picks her face and the back of her shoulders.
- She was sexually abused by the father of her mother's roommate.
- She has been in NC for 10 yrs. In paranoia, she disconnected from her family. At the end of Dec, she asked for forgiveness and reconnected with them.
- She has been attending church with her brother.
- She had been barricading herself in her room.
- She lost her boyfriend of 3 years because of her paranoia. She stated that he was "tired of her antics."
- Her children live in FL with their father. She left them there 4 years ago.
- She has an appt with Dr. ___ on 2/14 to discuss the Invega. She believes it is working. The paranoia has ceased. She still sees "shadow people."
- She stated that she cannot keep a relationship. No one can stand to live with her.
- She has been in and out of treatment since age 12.

Services Offered (check all that apply) — Recommended 30 min of exercise per day.
- X Continued counseling
- ___ Personality assessment
- ___ Information only
- ___ Single clinical contact
- ___ Referral to group/program (specify) manic now. She is experiencing
- ___ Other (specify) pressured speech.
- ___ Crisis intervention/consultation
- ___ Referral to outside agency/practitioner
- ___ Third party consultation — She stated
- ___ Psychiatric referral that she feels

Entry 37 - Initial Contact Report Continue

Social History (i.e., family, developmental, and psychiatric history & treatment for self and family):
She has an older brother and a younger sister. Her parents divorced when she was 4 yrs old. Her father was an alcoholic. She stayed with him when they divorced. Her mother has Bipolar disorder and used drugs. She dropped out of school at age 13. She got her GED at age 17 through the Job Corps.

Examinational Data (mental status; attitudes/moods/perceptions; thought process; memory; impulse; judgment):

Threat to Self: __X__ Low ____ Moderate ____ High
Comments/History: She has attempted suicide at least 3x. The last attempt was 8 years ago. Stated that she is not currently experiencing suicidal ideation.

Threat to Others: __X__ Low ____ Moderate ____ High
Comments/History: She was arrested for domestic violence in '98 (former husband) and '01 (her sister).

[?]

Diagnostic Impression and Case Conceptualization: Liberty endorsed a wide variety of symptoms on the checklist at intake. She described paranoia, anxiety, and visual hallucinations (shadow people) as the predominant issues. She has difficulty maintaining relationships. In Dec, she worked to repair family connection. She attributed family problems to her paranoia. Her mood was labile. She was well groomed and appropriately dressed. She has been seeing Dr. _____ for psychotropic medications. Reported that she is compliant w/ medications.

DSM-IV Diagnosis:	Axis I: 300.21 Panic Dis. w/ Agoraphobia 298.9 Psychotic Dis. NOS
	Axis II: Deferred
	Axis III: Migraines
	Axis IV: Inadequate Social Support; Relationship Difficulties
	Axis V: GAF = 48 (At Intake) Inadequate Finances

Plan/Recommendation: Recommended continued therapy and regular exercise of 30 min per day 5 days per week.

Therapist Signature

2-4-13
Date

Any Thoughts

Entry 38 – Home Therapist Note
Date: 02/14/2013

Session Information

Client:	Crouch, Liberty (
Staff:	Marty (
Service Date/Time:	2/14/2013 1:15 PM - 1:30 PM
Client Program:	
Activity:	
Organization:	
Service Location:	- Cruce

Goal(s) Addressed

No Goal(s) addressed were chosen

Goal(s) Addressed: To receive medication management and medication evaluation

REC Progress Note

INTERVENTION SECTION

Intervention: Issues/Symptoms/Challenges Processed; Recovery Skills/Tools/Techniques Taught

This was my first meeting with Liberty. She told me she has been in a manic phase for two months and believes she is coming down from it because her speech has slowed. She is concerned about what kind of low she might hit since this is the longest manic phase she has had. I offered her peer support to help monitor her depression and support her through it, and she said she would be happy for me to make some home visits since she isn't comfortable in the ▇▇▇ due to seeing people she used to use with.

Was a formal Risk Assessment done as part of this intervention?
○ Yes
○ No

OUTCOME SECTION

Outcome: How did the individual respond to the intervention named above? How is the individual progressing towards goals? What is the plan from here?

Liberty appeared comfortable talking with me, and shared some of her difficulties (paranoia, isolation). We plan to meet once a week to reduce her isolation and support her in self-understanding.

Student Status: Additional Learning About The Student: What did you learn about the student that others may need to know?

Signatures

Signature #1: Marty ▇▇▇ - 2/15/2013 10:14 AM

Signature History

Action	Date	Staff
Document Signed	2/15/2013	Marty

Liberty Crouch

Entry 39 – Psychiatrist Note
Date: 02/14/2013

Session Information

Client:	Crouch, Liberty
Staff:	Don
Service Date/Time:	2/14/2013 1:30 PM - 2:00 PM

Client Program:
Activity:

Organization:
Service Location: - Office

Medical Template

HPI: Liberty is here today for a recheck. She has stopped smoking. She did not really like the way she felt on her Invega and she has gained some weight which concerns her. She does not want to continue on this. She would like me to check a lesion on her foot that is developed over the past several months. It is asymptomatic.

She has an appointment on April 5 to see a neurologist regarding her headaches. She does continue taking Excedrin. Her headaches usually occur soon after waking up in the morning.

She is concerned because she feels like she has been an a low level mania since December.

Review of Systems: Denies any history of heart disease, chest pain, palpitations, edema. She reports a h/o HTN. Denies any dysuria or urinary frequency. Denies any diarrhea or rectal bleeding. She does have constipation. She does not take anything for this. Denies a history of hepatitis, cancer, or blood clots. She has had intermittant dizziness. Denies any numbness. Denies any cough or shortness of breath. Denies any double or blurred vision. Denies any recent weight gain or weight loss. Menses occur about twice a week. She is not sexually active.

PMHx: History of a thyroid abnormality 2 years ago that was never followed up on. She had some preliminary lab work showed a decreased TSH and a decreased free T4.
She has had 2 children. They both live with their father.

PSHx / PFHx: She lives alone. Her brother will help transport her. He lives nearby. She does smoke but is trying to stop. Her ex-boyfriend is also involved.

Strong family history of multiple family members having significant mental illness.

Objective: Blood pressure is 130/80. Pulse is 78 and regular. Weight is 125 pounds. (Which is up 7 pounds) Neck without thyromegaly or lymphadenopathy. Lungs sounds are clear bilaterally. Heart is regular rate and rhythm without murmur. Gait is normal. She is calm and conversant today.

Data Reviewed: Recent lab work including her I would studies was normal. I reviewed this with her today.

Assessment / Plan: 1. Schizoaffective disorder with intolerance to Invega. She has taken some of the other atypical antipsychotics and did not like them. She also did not do well on Depakote in the past. She does not think that she has tried Tegretol or Neurontin as a mood stabilizer. She does continue on Topamax. I will add Tegretol 200 mg b.i.d. Follow up with me in one-2 months. She will call sooner with problems. She seems to be fairly sensitive to medications.

2. Hypertension. This appears to be stable. She continues on clonidine.

3. History of hyperthyroidism. Thyroid tests are now normal.

4. Nicotine dependence. Now abstaining.

Tests Ordered:

Entry 40 – Psychologist Note
Date: 02/18/2013
2 Days Before My Great Deliverance

PROGRESS NOTES

Appearance/Dress: ☒ Appropriate ☐ Other _____ **Affect:** ☐ Congruent ☒ Other _Labile_

Behavior: ☐ Appropriate ☐ Guarded ☒ Restless ☐ Pacing ☐ Threatening ☐ Responds to Structure ☐ Passive
☐ Helpless/Hopeless ☐ Responsive to interp ☐ Resists interp ☐ Speech logical/coherent ☐ Other _____

Mental Status: ☒ Oriented Person/Place/Time ☒ Alert ☒ Tracks conversation ☒ Memory intact ☐ Memory impaired
☐ Sedate/Confused/Unable to follow directions ☐ Other _____

Thought content: ☒ Concrete/Abstract/Insightful ☐ Disorganized/Tangential/LOA/Ideas of Reference ☐ Suspicious/Paranoid _of people breaking in her home_
☐ Hallucinations/Delusions ☐ Blames self ☐ Blames others ☐ Other _____

Judgment: ☒ Appropriate ☐ Limited/Inconsistent/Poor ☐ Other _____

Safety: ~~Denied~~ Suicidal/Homicidal/Self-Harm ☐ Plan: _____ ☐ Means: _____
☐ Support System: Available/Not available ☐ Contract for Safety

Notes/Plan: I saw Liberty for a regularly scheduled 60-minute session. We continued CBT for
- She is on the 3rd day of Pegretol instead of Invega
- She is experiencing paranoia. Stated that she is also anxious. She is nauseous and has been having difficulty sleeping.
- She uses prayer to handle her fears.
- She fasts on Sunday and does not talk to anyone on that day. She texts her children. Her boyfriend was jealous when she would not answer her door.
- She is exhausted.
- Having difficulty making decisions. She gave an ex of having trouble deciding what to wear to bed although she lives alone.
- She is attending a class called "Transforming You" at church on Wednesday. It is helping her change her relationships with her children.
- Stated that her dreams are important to her. She stated that they are vivid.
- Her next appt is March 6 @ 2:00pm

Date: 2/18/13 **Length of Session:** 1hr **Clinician:** Lynne

> Did I cancel this appointment? Where is the missing file? I do remember playing in your sandbox.

Question Doc?
Did I cancel this appt? Where is the missing file? I do remember playing in your sandbox.

Patient Name: Liberty Crouch **DOB:** _____ **Date:** 2/18/13
Lynne **Copayment Amount:** 0 **Session Time:** 11:00 am

Liberty Crouch

~ 138 ~

Entry 41 – Home Therapist Note
Date: 02/20/2013
The Morning of My Great Deliverance

Entry

Session Information

Client:	Crouch, Liberty
Staff:	Marty
Service Date/Time:	2/20/2013 9:00 AM - 11:00 AM
Client Program:	
Activity:	
Organization:	
Service Location:	Place of Service

Goal(s) Addressed

No Goal(s) addressed were chosen

Goal(s) Addressed: medication management and evaluation

REC Progress Note

INTERVENTION SECTION

Intervention: Issues/Symptoms/Challenges Processed, Recovery Skills/Tools/Techniques Taught

Liberty told me about her struggles and about the things that work for her. She told me that she had been manic for two months and was sliding into a depression. Liberty isolates except for church, but she agreed to accept my support in her depression and allow me to help her monitor her emotions. Her art (photography and poetry) and her religious faith help her deal with her depression and isolation.

Was a formal Risk Assessment done as part of this intervention?
○ Yes
○ No

OUTCOME SECTION

Outcome: How did the individual respond to the intervention named above? How is the individual progressing towards goals? What is the plan from here?

Liberty and I have planned that we will spend some time together weekly, with some extra phone support while she is in this depressive state. Her medication was adjusted recently, and she will give me regular feedback on how she feels it is working.

Student Status: Additional Learning About The Student: What did you learn about the student that others may need to know?

Signatures

Signature #1: Marty — 2/21/2013 9:06 PM

Signature History

Action	Date	Staff
Document Signed	2/21/2013	Marty

Demons Release Trilogies, Book 3

~ 139 ~

Entry 42 – Home Therapist Note
Date: 02/27/2013
7 Days After My Great Deliverance

Session Information

Client:	Crouch, Liberty
Staff:	Marty
Service Date/Time:	2/27/2013 9:30 AM - 11:00 AM

Client Program:	
Activity:	
Organization:	
Service Location:	- Other Place of Service

Goal(s) Addressed

No Goal(s) addressed were chosen

Goal(s) Addressed: to receive medication management and medication evaluation

REC Progress Note

INTERVENTION SECTION

Intervention: Issues/Symptoms/Challenges Processed; Recovery Skills/Tools/Techniques Taught

I drove Liberty to _____ to apply for rent assistance. She was in a cheerful mood, and said that the depression she was in left her after she was anointed by the pastors at her church last week. She also said that she has been able to sleep at night and not be plagued by fears of someone breaking in to her appt. She was excited because her son's father has offered to buy her a plane ticket to come to Fla. for her son's b-day in March. The application process at _____ went smoothly. I asked if she was taking her medications regularly, and she said "Yes I am. God has given me the tools to heal myself."

Was a formal Risk Assessment done as part of this intervention?
○ Yes
○ No

OUTCOME SECTION

Outcome: How did the individual respond to the intervention named above? How is the individual progressing towards goals? What is the plan from here?

Liberty said she would like to continue seeing me on a weekly basis. She said that she needs regular contact with someone who will help her monitor her mood disorder.

Student Status: Additional Learning About The Student What did you learn about the student that others may need to know?

Signatures

Signature #1: Marty _____ - 2/27/2013 3:05 PM

Signature History

Action	Date	Staff
Document Signed	2/27/2013	Marty

Liberty Crouch

Any Thoughts

Entry 43 – Home Therapist Note
Date: 03/08/2013

Session Information

Client:	Crouch, Liberty
Staff:	Marty
Service Date/Time:	3/8/2013 9:00 AM - 10:00 AM
Client Program:	
Activity:	
Organization:	
Service Location:	Other Place of Service

Goal(s) Addressed

REC Treatment Plan

Problem	Depression
Goal	To receive medication management and medication evaluation

Goal(s) Addressed:

REC Progress Note

INTERVENTION SECTION

Intervention: Issues/Symptoms/Challenges Processed; Recovery Skills/Tools/Techniques Taught

I took Liberty to the pharmacy to pick up a prescription. We talked about her plans for her Florida trip. She is excited about going, but somewhat concerned because she was unable to be baptized on the 3rd (she was snowed in), and she is worried that the "demons might try to reenter me." I suggested that she continue her prayer and Bible readings and keep her faith strong since that is what has been giving her a sense of balance and joy.

Was a formal Risk Assessment done as part of this intervention?
○ Yes
○ No

OUTCOME SECTION

Outcome: How did the individual respond to the intervention named above? How is the individual progressing towards goals? What is the plan from here?

I will meet with Liberty when she comes back from Florida in April. We agreed that she will call me if she feels a need for support. "I am blessed to have you," she said. "I don't like being around people, and I feel safe with you."

Student Status:
Additional Learning About The Student: What did you learn about the student that others may need to know?

Signatures

Signature #1: Marty - 3/11/2013 10:29 AM

Signature History

Liberty Crouch

Entry 44 – Home Therapist Note
Date: 04/02/2013

Session Information

Client:	Crouch, Liberty
Staff:	, Marty
Service Date/Time:	4/2/2013 9:00 AM - 11:00 AM

Client Program:
Activity:
Organization:
Service Location: , - Other Place of Service

Goal(s) Addressed

No Goal(s) addressed were chosen

Goal(s) Addressed: | Peer support for depression/anxiety

REC Progress Note

INTERVENTION SECTION

Intervention: | Issues/Symptoms/Challenges Processed; Recovery Skills/Tools/Techniques Taught

Liberty had finished the medication for blood pressure, and wondered if she needed to get it refilled. With Dr. input, I brought Liberty to and checked her BP. It was a healthy 120/80, indicating that at this time, a refill isn't necessary. We returned to her house where she read me journal entries about her recovery journey and discussed the direction she feels she is moving toward.

Was a formal Risk Assessment done as part of this intervention? | ○ Yes
○ No

OUTCOME SECTION

Outcome: | How did the individual respond to the intervention named above? How is the individual progressing towards goals? What is the plan from here?

Liberty's son has come to live with her. He is having some problems, which may add to Liberty's anxiety, but overall, it seems that having the ability to act on her maternal instincts is having a positive effect for Liberty.

Student Status:
Additional Learning About The Student: | What did you learn about the student that others may need to know?

Signatures

Signature #1: | Marty   4/2/2013 11:51 AM

Signature History

Action	Date	Staff
Document Signed	4/2/2013	Marty

Demons Release Trilogies, Book 3

~ 143 ~

Entry 45 – Home Therapist Note
Date: 04/08/2013

Session Information

Client:	Crouch, Liberty
Staff:	, Marty
Service Date/Time:	4/8/2013 10:15 AM – 12:30 PM

Client Program:	
Activity:	
Organization:	
Service Location:	Other Place of Service

Goal(s) Addressed

No Goal(s) addressed were chosen

Goal(s) Addressed:

REC Progress Note

INTERVENTION SECTION

Intervention: Issues/Symptoms/Challenges Processed; Recovery Skills/Tools/Techniques Taught

Liberty is happy that her 18 yr. old son has come to live with her, and she is adjusting well to the changes. She has a washer hook-up in her apt, so we shopped 2nd hand stores to find her an inexpensive washer. Liberty has figured that she will save enough laundrymat money to cover the cost of the washer, since her son is active in school and sports. She has also budgeted for healthy meals for herself and her son, and I took her grocery shopping and made recomendations based on my experience of raising two boys.

Was a formal Risk Assessment done as part of this intervention?
○ Yes
○ No

OUTCOME SECTION

Outcome: How did the individual respond to the intervention named above? How is the individual progressing towards goals? What is the plan from here?

Liberty is always grateful to have any assistance, whether it is listening to her discuss issues in her life or being s sounding board for ideas or providing transportation and companionship. I will be taking her later this week to enroll her son in high school here.

Student Status: Additional Learning About The Student: What did you learn about the student that others may need to know?

Signatures

Signature #1. | Marty   - 4/10/2013 12:28 PM

Signature History

Action	Date	Staff
Document Signed	4/10/2013	Marty

Liberty Crouch

Entry 46 – Psychiatrist Note
Date: 04/08/2013

Session Information

Client:	Crouch, Liberty (
Staff:	, Don (
Service Date/Time:	4/8/2013 2:00 PM - 2:30 PM
Client Program:	
Activity:	
Organization:	
Service Location:	- Office

Medical Template

HPI: Liberty is here for a recheck on her overall condition. She did recently see the neurologist who increased her Topamax to 75 mg b.i.d.

Since her last visit she went to the emergency room on one occasion when her blood pressure was elevated at the OB/GYN office. She was started on lisinopril but has since stopped that. Her blood pressure is doing fine without it. She was anxious at that time that her blood pressure was elevated.

She feels that her mood is much better taking Tegretol b.i.d. for her schizoaffective disorder. She has no side effects to the medicine.

Review of Systems: Denies any history of heart disease, chest pain, palpitations, edema. She reports a h/o HTN. Denies any dysuria or urinary frequency. Denies any diarrhea or rectal bleeding. She does have constipation. She does not take anything for this. Denies a history of hepatitis, cancer, or blood clots. She has had intermittent dizziness. Denies any numbness. Denies any cough or shortness of breath. Denies any double or blurred vision. Denies any recent weight gain or weight loss. Menses occur about twice a week. She is not sexually active.

PMHx: History of a thyroid abnormality 2 years ago that was never followed up on. She had some preliminary lab work showed a decreased TSH and a decreased free T4.

She has had 2 children. They both live with their father.

PSHx / PFHx: She lives alone. Her brother will help transport her. He lives nearby. She does smoke but is trying to stop. Her ex-boyfriend is also involved.

Strong family history of multiple family members having significant mental illness.

Objective: Blood pressure is 138/80. Pulse is 78 and regular. Weight is 121 pounds. Neck without thyromegaly or lymphadenopathy. Lungs sounds are clear bilaterally. Heart is regular rate and rhythm without murmur. Gait is normal. She is calm and conversant today. She looks very good. Her mood is very bright.

Data Reviewed:

> Note: I actually have a 3rd child, didn't know if you heard? 😊 Just Sayin!

Assessment / Plan:
1. Schizoaffective disorder. She appears to be doing much better and her Tegretol. I will continue this. She will take 200 mg b.i.d.

2. Hypertension. This appears to be controlled well with clonidine. She does have times when he gets easily elevated when she is anxious or upset. Continue same dose for now. She will remain off of her lisinopril.

3. Migraine headaches. Continue follow up with her neurologist. Continue Topamax and Imitrex p.r.n.

Tests Ordered: None at this time.

Vitals Entry

Date: 04/08/2013
02:15 PM

Entry 47 - Vitals Check Note
Date: 04/08/2013

Blood Pressure: 138 / 80
Heart Rate:
Respiration Rate:
Temperature: Fahrenheit
Height: Inches 61.5
Weight: Pounds 121
BMI: 22.49
Pain Scale:

Additional Services

Setting: ○ Inpatient ● Outpatient
Client Status: ○ New Patient ● Existing Patient ○ Consultation
Was >50% of time used for counseling: ○ Yes ● No
Total Psychotherapy time (minutes):

Evaluation and Management Calculator

History Type	Exam Type	MDM Type
○ None	○ None	○ None
○ Problem Focused	○ Problem Focused	○ Straightforward
○ Expanded Problem Focused	○ Expanded Problem Focused	● Low Complexity
● Detailed	● Detailed	○ Moderate Complexity
○ Comprehensive	○ Comprehensive	○ High Complexity

E/M Level: 4

Signatures

Signature #1: Don - 4/11/2013 10:39 AM

Signature History

Action	Date	Staff
Document Signed	4/11/2013	Don

Liberty Crouch

Any Thoughts

Entry 48 - Home Therapist Note
Date: 04/10/2013

Session Information

Client:	Crouch, Liberty
Staff:	Marty
Service Date/Time:	4/10/2013 8:30 AM - 11:00 AM

Client Program:
Activity:
Organization:
Service Location: Place of Service

Goal(s) Addressed

No Goal(s) addressed were chosen

Goal(s) Addressed: | Continued recovery

REC Progress Note

INTERVENTION SECTION

Intervention: | Issues/Symptoms/Challenges Processed; Recovery Skills/Tools/Techniques Taught

I provided transportation for Liberty to go to ___ High and the alternate school to enroll her son in classes. She is setting him up to get caught up in school, be eligible for football. During drive time, I assisted Liberty in brainstorming possibilities for transportation for her son to get to his schools because they are both out of his district.

Was a formal Risk Assessment done as part of this intervention?
○ Yes
○ No

OUTCOME SECTION

Outcome: | How did the individual respond to the intervention named above? How is the individual progressing towards goals? What is the plan from here?

I supported Liberty in managing anxiety as she helps her son make appropriate choices. "I basically quit school when I was a kid...I want better for my son." Liberty demonstrates that she is striving to make the right choices not just for her son, but for herself and her continued recovery.

Student Status:
Additional Learning About The Student: | What did ___ rn about the student that others may need to know?

Signatures

Signature #1: | Marty   - 4/12/2013 11:59 AM

Signature History

Action	Date	Staff
Document Signed	4/12/2013	Marty

Liberty Crouch

Entry 49 – Home Therapist Note
Date: 04/24/2013

Session Information

Client:	Crouch, Liberty ( )
Staff:	Marty
Service Date/Time:	4/24/2013 8:15 AM - 8:45 AM
Client Program:	
Activity:	
Organization:	
Service Location:	- Other Place of Service

Goal(s) Addressed

No Goal(s) addressed were chosen

Goal(s) Addressed: support

REC Progress Note

INTERVENTION SECTION

Intervention: Issues/Symptoms/Challenges Processed; Recovery Skills/Tools/Techniques Taught

Liberty called last night very anxious because she had a meeting at her son's school for 8:30 this morning and her transportation had fallen through. I was able to step in and provide the transportation. We talked about the responsibilities of parenting and how to juggle self care with meeting the needs of our kids.

Was a formal Risk Assessment done as part of this intervention?
○ Yes
○ No

OUTCOME SECTION

Outcome: How did the individual respond to the intervention named above? How is the individual progressing towards goals? What is the plan from here?

Liberty expressed her gratitude. "I thank you more than you know." She said she was able to let the anxiety go last night knowing that she could make the appointment.

Student Status:
Additional Learning About The Student: What did you learn about the student that others may need to know?

Signatures

Signature #1: | Marty   4/24/2013 11:01 AM

Signature History

Action	Date	Staff
Document Signed	4/24/2013	Marty

Demons Release Trilogies, Book 3

~ 149 ~

Entry 50 – Home Therapist Note
Date: 05/03/2013

Session Information

Client:	Crouch, Liberty
Staff:	Marty
Service Date/Time:	5/3/2013 10:00 AM - 11:00 AM

Client Program:	
Activity:	
Organization:	
Service Location:	- Other Place of Service

Goal(s) Addressed

No Goal(s) addressed were chosen

Goal(s) Addressed: Integrated Care

REC Progress Note

INTERVENTION SECTION

Intervention: Issues/Symptoms/Challenges Processed; Recovery Skills/Tools/Techniques Taught

When Liberty's son came to live with her, she put a used washing machine on layaway b/c she knew it would help them save money in the long run (transit & laundromat costs). The store was ready to deliver and install the machine but first, Liberty needed to pay it off. I took her to the bank to get the money to do so.

Was a formal Risk Assessment done as part of this intervention?
○ Yes
○ No

OUTCOME SECTION

Outcome: How did the individual respond to the intervention named above? How is the individual progressing towards goals? What is the plan from here?

With her limited income, Liberty does a good job of budgeting and prioritizing. I affirmed her financial decisions, and we shared, "mom to mom" about the additional joys and stressors of having young adult sons.

Student Status: Additional Learning About The Student: What did you learn about the student that others may need to know?

Signatures

Signature #1: Marty - 5/10/2013 9:52 AM

Signature History

Action	Date	Staff
Document Signed	5/10/2013	Marty

Liberty Crouch

~ 150 ~

Entry 51 – Home Therapist Note
Date: 05/07/2013

Session Information

Client: Crouch, Liberty
Staff: Marty
Service Date/Time: 5/7/2013 1:15 PM - 3:00 PM

Client Program:
Activity:
Organization:
Service Location: Other Place of Service

Goal(s) Addressed

No Goal(s) addressed were chosen

Goal(s) Addressed:

REC Progress Note

INTERVENTION SECTION

Intervention: Issues/Symptoms/Challenges Processed; Recovery Skills/Tools/Techniques Taught

Liberty needed transportation and support for her anxiety for a trip to ▆▆. The wait to see a case worker was considerable, and I had light conversation with Liberty to help ease her discomfort. Liberty had previously asked if I would accompany her to the supermarket, but by the time she finished at ▆▆, she said "I need to go home to my safe spot. I've used up all my courage."

Was a formal Risk Assessment done as part of this intervention?
○ Yes
○ No

OUTCOME SECTION

Outcome: How did the individual respond to the intervention named above? How is the individual progressing towards goals? What is the plan from here?

Liberty uses coping skills that work for her - preparing herself mentally by praying for strength and walking through the task in her mind. When she starts to feel the stress of being away from home, she becomes agitated and starts to feel hostile toward the world. I will work with her on some grounding exercises, and when possible, make use of her spiritual practices.

Student Status:
Additional Learning About The Student: What did you learn about the student that others may need to know?

Signatures

Signature #1: Marty - 5/13/2013 10:29 AM

Signature History

Action	Date	Staff
Document Signed	5/13/2013	Marty

Demons Release Trilogies, Book 3

~ 151 ~

Entry 52 - Home Therapist Note
Date: 05/10/2013

Session Information

Client: Crouch, Liberty
Staff: Marty
Service Date/Time: 5/10/2013 12:00 PM - 2:15 PM

Client Program:
Activity:
Organization:
Service Location: Other Place of Service

Goal(s) Addressed

No Goal(s) addressed were chosen

Goal(s) Addressed:

REC Progress Note

INTERVENTION SECTION

Intervention: Issues/Symptoms/Challenges Processed; Recovery Skills/Tools/Techniques Taught

Liberty wanted support for shopping. She is becoming more comfortable with one of the area supermarkets, and asked to go there. She said now that she is learning the store's layout and making lists to fit that layout helps her with anxiety reduction.

Was a formal Risk Assessment done as part of this intervention?
○ Yes
○ No

OUTCOME SECTION

Outcome: How did the individual respond to the intervention named above? How is the individual progressing towards goals? What is the plan from here?

Liberty said that she is beginning to build up more confidence in attending to outside needs.

Student Status:
Additional Learning About The Student: What did you learn about the student that others may need to know?

Signatures

Signature #1: Marty   5/13/2013 11:37 AM

Signature History

Action	Date	Staff
Document Signed	5/13/2013	Marty

Liberty Crouch

Any Thoughts

~ 153 ~

Entry 53 – Home Therapist Note
Date: 05/15/2013

Session Information

Client:	Crouch, Liberty
Staff:	Marty
Service Date/Time:	5/15/2013 12:30 PM - 1:30 PM

Client Program:	
Activity:	
Organization:	
Service Location:	- Other Place of Service

Goal(s) Addressed

No Goal(s) addressed were chosen

Goal(s) Addressed:

REC Progress Note

INTERVENTION SECTION

Intervention: Issues/Symptoms/Challenges Processed; Recovery Skills/Tools/Techniques Taught

Liberty needed to pick up her medications. After we got the meds, we took a walk, and she talked about becoming emotionally ready to share some of her poetry in a public venue. (A poetry club in ____) I encouraged her to pursue this. She asked if I could come and be part of her support system the first time she goes, and I told her I would be happy to, and reflected the growth I've seen in her in a few months time.

Was a formal Risk Assessment done as part of this intervention?
○ Yes
○ No

OUTCOME SECTION

Outcome: How did the individual respond to the intervention named above? How is the individual progressing towards goals? What is the plan from here?

Liberty is using her religious faith to help guide her and give her strength, and she acknowledges that she will have to push her comfort zones to have the life "God wants for me."

Student Status: Additional Learning About The Student: What did you learn about the student that others may need to know?

Signatures

Signature #1: Marty - 5/16/2013 11:53 AM

Signature History

Action	Date	Staff
Document Signed	5/16/2013	Marty

Liberty Crouch

Entry 54 – Home Therapist Note
Date: 05/22/2013

Session Information

Client:	Crouch, Liberty
Staff:	Marty
Service Date/Time:	5/22/2013 10:30 AM - 12:00 PM
Client Program:	
Activity:	
Organization:	
Service Location:	- Other Place of Service

Goal(s) Addressed

No Goal(s) addressed were chosen

Goal(s) Addressed:

REC Progress Note

INTERVENTION SECTION

Intervention: Issues/Symptoms/Challenges Processed; Recovery Skills/Tools/Techniques Taught

Liberty needed assistance getting some materials ready for a book she is writing about her recovery from trauma, mental illness and substance abuse. We went to ▓▓▓ to get some copies made, then came to the ▓▓▓ to sign releases to get her medical records. Liberty shared with me that she had been given some meth this week and had thoughts of using it, but flushed it instead. "I lied about it, I thought about what it would feel like, I was on the verge of relapse, but I realized that it was the devil tempting me, so I prayed and overcame evil." I praised her choice and her inner strength.

Was a formal Risk Assessment done as part of this intervention?
○ Yes
○ No

OUTCOME SECTION

Outcome: How did the individual respond to the intervention named above? How is the individual progressing towards goals? What is the plan from here?

Liberty will meet with Katie to go over her records when they are released. I gave her a forewarning that there may be some things written in her records that can be upsetting.

Student Status: Additional Learning About The Student: What did you learn about the student that others may need to know?

Signatures

Signature #1: Marty) - 5/22/2013 2:08 PM

Signature History

Action	Date	Staff
Document Signed	5/22/2013	Marty

Note: Refer to Part III – The Lamb – A Test: I Let the Devil in My House

Demons Release Trilogies, Book 3

~ 155 ~

Entry 55 – Home Therapist Note
Date: 05/28/2013

Session Information

Client:	Crouch, Liberty
Staff:	Marty
Service Date/Time:	5/28/2013 1:30 PM - 3:30 PM
Client Program:	
Activity:	
Organization:	
Service Location:	- Office

Goal(s) Addressed

No Goal(s) addressed were chosen

Goal(s) Addressed:

REC Progress Note

INTERVENTION SECTION

Intervention: Issues/Symptoms/Challenges Processed; Recovery Skills/Tools/Techniques Taught

Liberty has not had problems with her migraines lately, which I find interesting since she has been doing so much soul-searching work on her autobiography and I had thought that might trigger a migraine. The converse is true - she claims to be happier and more balanced. I took Liberty to various health care providers to arrange for her to gain access to her medical records because she wants to make sure she is truthful in her writing. I supported Liberty through this process with motivational interviewing techniques.

Was a formal Risk Assessment done as part of this intervention?
○ Yes
○ No

OUTCOME SECTION

Outcome: How did the individual respond to the intervention named above? How is the individual progressing towards goals? What is the plan from here?

Liberty feels so directed at this time that she believes she is strong enough to get a part time job. She has applied for a housekeeping job at a restaurant, going in in the mornings to clean the dining room and bathrooms. She laughed "that fits right in with my OCD!" The biggest advantage for her is that she would be working at a time when the restaurant would be empty, so her fear of being around people wouldn't surface.

Student Status: Additional Learning About The Student: What did you learn about the student that others may need to know?

Signatures

Signature #1: Marty   5/29/2013 9:28 AM

Signature History

Action	Date	Staff
Document Signed	5/29/2013	Marty

Liberty Crouch

Entry 56 – Home Therapist Note
Date: 05/31/2013

Session Information

Client:	Crouch, Liberty
Staff:	MARTY
Service Date/Time:	5/31/2013 9:15 AM - 10:15 AM
Client Program:	
Activity:	
Organization:	
Service Location:	Other Place of Service

Goal(s) Addressed

No Goal(s) addressed were chosen

Goal(s) Addressed:

REC Progress Note

INTERVENTION SECTION

Intervention: Issues/Symptoms/Challenges Processed, Recovery Skills/Tools/Techniques Taught

Liberty and I went to Lake _____ to walk. "This will be good for both of us," she said. We walked at a fairly quick pace and talked about parenting young adults and strategies for doing the best job we can. We also talked about how, at some point, we have to let go and let them make their own mistakes. I shared some of the things I had learned in my own recovery work on codependence

Was a formal Risk Assessment done as part of this intervention?
○ Yes
○ No

OUTCOME SECTION

Outcome: How did the individual respond to the intervention named above? How is the individual progressing towards goals? What is the plan from here?

Liberty said the conversations had helped her. "I always rescued my son, and I see how that is now a problem for us." She intends to work on stepping back from helping him make choices while continuing to hold him accountable for his responsibilities.

Student Status:
Additional Learning About The Student: What did you learn about the student that others may need to know?

Signatures

Signature #1: Marty - 5/31/2013 2:44 PM

Signature History

Action	Date	Staff
Document Signed	5/31/2013	Marty

Demons Release Trilogies, Book 3

~ 157 ~

Entry 57 – Home Therapist Note
Date: 06/03/2013

Session Information

Client:	Crouch, Liberty
Staff:	Marty
Service Date/Time:	6/3/2013 10:00 AM - 1:00 PM
Client Program:	
Activity:	
Organization:	
Service Location:	- Other Place of Service

Goal(s) Addressed

No Goal(s) addressed were chosen

Goal(s) Addressed:

REC Progress Note

INTERVENTION SECTION

Intervention: Issues/Symptoms/Challenges Processed; Recovery Skills/Tools/Techniques Taught

Liberty and I walked around Lake ___. "I know I look tiny," she said, "but I'm actually really out of shape and soft. I need this exercise." She talked about her faith beliefs and how they keep her strong. "I know all the answers I need are in the Bible." She said she believes that God has given her ___ and her doctors to help her get well, and now that she is getting better, it will be her turn to give to others. After our walk, we picked up her medicines and some groceries.

Was a formal Risk Assessment done as part of this intervention?
○ Yes
○ No

OUTCOME SECTION

Outcome: How did the individual respond to the intervention named above? How is the individual progressing towards goals? What is the plan from here?

Liberty said she still isn't comfortable being around people, but I notice how friendly she is with people walking around the lake. However, when she goes into a grocery store or the pharmacy, she becomes very focused and appears tenser. I will work with her on some grounding exercises she can use while in the store that might help.

Student Status: Additional Learning About The Student: What did you learn about the student that others may need to know?

Signatures

Signature #1: Marty   6/4/2013 4:33 PM

Signature History

Action	Date	Staff
Document Signed	6/4/2013	Marty

Liberty Crouch

Any Thoughts

~ 159 ~

Entry 58 – Home Therapist Note
Date: 06/05/2013 Accepting the Doctor Reports as a Part of My Past

Session Information

Client:	Crouch, Liberty
Staff:	Marty
Service Date/Time:	6/5/2013 8:30 AM - 9:00 AM
Client Program:	
Activity:	
Organization:	
Service Location:	- Office

Goal(s) Addressed

No Goal(s) addressed were chosen

Goal(s) Addressed:

REC Progress Note

INTERVENTION SECTION

Intervention: Issues/Symptoms/Challenges Processed; Recovery Skills/Tools/Techniques Taught

Liberty had an appt. with Kate to review her psychiatric/counseling records. I provided transportation to ___ and emotional support for the review.

Was a formal Risk Assessment done as part of this intervention?
○ Yes
○ No

OUTCOME SECTION

Outcome: How did the individual respond to the intervention named above? How is the individual progressing towards goals? What is the plan from here?

Liberty brought her anxiety medication "just in case I become overwhelmed." She did not need to use it; she had several questions but accepted her records as a part of her past.

Student Status: Additional Learning About The Student: What did you learn about the student that others may need to know?

Signatures

Signature #1: Marty -- 6/6/2013 9:29 AM

Signature History

Action	Date	Staff
Document Signed	6/6/2013	Marty

Liberty Crouch

Entry 59 – Continued Home Therapist Note
Date: 06/05/2013

Session Information

Client:	Crouch, Liberty
Staff:	Marty
Service Date/Time:	6/5/2013 11:00 AM - 11:30 AM
Client Program:	
Activity:	
Organization:	
Service Location:	- Other Place of Service

Goal(s) Addressed

No Goal(s) addressed were chosen

Goal(s) Addressed:

REC Progress Note

INTERVENTION SECTION

Intervention: Issues/Symptoms/Challenges Processed, Recovery Skills/Tools/Techniques Taught
Transportation for trip home. Discussed my records with Liberty, and she has requested a copy of them.

Was a formal Risk Assessment done as part of this intervention?
○ Yes
○ No

OUTCOME SECTION

Outcome: How did the individual respond to the intervention named above? How is the individual progressing towards goals? What is the plan from here?
I will deliver my records to Liberty on Friday when we have a walk scheduled.

Student Status:
Additional Learning About The Student: What did you learn about the student that others may need to know?

Signatures

Signature #1: Marty - 6/6/2013 9:31 AM

Signature History

Action	Date	Staff
Document Signed	6/6/2013	Marty

Demons Release Trilogies, Book 3

~ 161 ~

Entry 60 – Home Therapist Note
Date: 06/07/2013 Sounds Hopeful

Session Information

Client:	Crouch, Liberty
Staff:	Marty
Service Date/Time:	6/7/2013 9:00 AM - 10:30 AM
Client Program:	
Activity:	
Organization:	
Service Location:	Other Place of Service

Goal(s) Addressed

No Goal(s) addressed were chosen

Goal(s) Addressed:

REC Progress Note

INTERVENTION SECTION

Intervention: Issues/Symptoms/Challenges Processed; Recovery Skills/Tools/Techniques Taught

Liberty needed support for her grocery shopping. She demonstrates knowledge of healthy eating and budgeting skills.

Was a formal Risk Assessment done as part of this intervention?
○ Yes
○ No

OUTCOME SECTION

Outcome: How did the individual respond to the intervention named above? How is the individual progressing towards goals? What is the plan from here?

Liberty consistently applies the wellness tools that work for her, and with her open-mindedness to learn more about her "disorders", I believe she will continue to grow in her recovery.

Student Status: Additional Learning About The Student: What did you learn about the student that others may need to know?

Signatures

Signature #1: Marty   6/10/2013 10:38 AM

Signature History

Action	Date	Staff
Document Signed	6/10/2013	Marty

Liberty Crouch

Entry 61 – The Vein of Love
Date of Surgery: 08/10/2010

Report Name: OPERATIVE REPORT Status Description: Draft
Event Date: 08/10/2010 00:00 Facility:
  Source:

Report Text

PATIENT NAME: CROUCH, LIBERTY ROOM NUMBER:
MEDICAL RECORD NUMBER: DATE OF ADMISSION:
DATE OF BIRTH:

DATE OF OPERATION: 08/10/2010

INDICATION FOR SURGERY
This is a 31-year-old female who presents complaining of painful, firm, tender left breast. The patient had previous sub glandular implants in the past, now is complaining of some pain and firmness consistent with capsular contracture of the left breast. The patient is indicated for exchange of the breast implants with capsulectomy of the left breast. The patient has been advised of the risks and complications including but not limited to infection, bleeding, scarring, possible need for further reconstructive surgery, possible residual functional or cosmetic deformity of the breasts. The patient was told that she might require a breast lift but refuses to have a breast lift at this time due to the vertical scars below the nipple. The patient otherwise understands and agrees to plan.

PREOPERATIVE DIAGNOSIS
Capsular contracture left breast.

POSTOPERATIVE DIAGNOSIS
Capsular contracture left breast.

PROCEDURE
Exchange of bilateral breast implants, capsulectomy left breast.

ANESTHESIA
General.

SURGEON

PROCEDURE
With the patient in the supine position, after the induction of general anesthesia, the breast area was prepped and draped in the usual sterile manner. Attention was then turned to the right breast where, through the previous inframammary crease incision, the right breast tissue was incised deep to the underlying capsule. The capsule was opened, the breast implant was removed, noted to be intact. The pocket was copiously irrigated with antibiotic saline and capsulotomy incisions were made in the capsule. The pectoralis muscle was elevated off the inferior rib margin and elevated up to the area of the clavicle creating a sub-muscular pocket extending from the medial sternal border to the anterior axillary line laterally. The pocket was further irrigated with copious amounts of antibiotic saline. A silicone gel high profile Mentor implant, reference #350-4004BC was inserted, 400 mL volume. This was done after evaluation with an implant sizer for size and contour. The wound was temporarily closed with #3-0 nylon suture. In a similar fashion the same procedure was performed on the left breast. However, moderate amount of firm capsular tissue was removed over the area of the previous firmness, consistent with a partial capsulectomy and the implant was removed and replaced in the sub-muscular plane as previously dictated with a similar silicone implant. The wound was temporarily closed. The patient was placed in a sitting position. Good

Entry 62 – The Vein of Love Continued

symmetry was noted. The patient was placed back in the supine position. The wounds were closed using #2-0 Chromic at the capsule level, #3-0 Chromic at the subcutaneous level, and #3-0 Monocryl in a running fashion at the skin level. Steri-Strips, gauze dressings, and a conforming bra were placed. An Ace bandage was also wrapped around the superior pole of both breasts circumferentially to keep the implants in place and the patient arrived to recovery in stable condition. Estimated blood loss is 50 mL.

Entry 63 – The Vein of Love
Description of Procedure

PATIENT NAME: CROUCH, LIBERTY   ROOM NUMBER:

MEDICAL RECORD NUMBER: DATE OF ADMISSION:

DATE OF BIRTH:

DATE OF SURGERY: 09/22/2010

INDICATIONS FOR THE SURGERY
This is a 31-year-old female, who presents with excess skin and bilateral ptoses of both breasts following the exchange of breast implants. Due to redundant skin in both breasts and the bilateral ptoses, the patient is indicated for a bilateral mastopexy. The patient has been advised of risks and complications including but not limited to infection, bleeding, scarring, possible need for further reconstructive surgery, possible residual asymmetry between both breasts, and possible numbness of the breasts or nipples. The patient understands and agrees to plan.

PREOPERATIVE DIAGNOSIS
Bilateral breast ptoses following exchange of bilateral breast implants.

POSTOPERATIVE DIAGNOSIS
Bilateral breast ptoses following exchange of bilateral breast implants.

PROCEDURE
Bilateral mastopexy.

SURGEON

ANESTHESIA
General.

DESCRIPTION OF PROCEDURE
With the patient in the supine position and after induction of general anesthesia preoperatively, the new nipple positions were marked 1 cm to 2 cm above the superior areolar edge with the patient in the sitting position. A periareolar vertical scar mastopexy was performed. The large nipple areola on the right and left side were both incised to 4 cm in diameter and skin incisions were made circumscribing the areola starting from the new positions superior to the areola and extending inferiorly approximately 6 cm below the areola. The vertical mastopexy was performed by removing a wedge of skin within the central area below the areola and undermining the wound margins. The wound margins were then brought together and sutured temporarily with a nipple areola in its new position, and the patient was placed in the sitting position. This was performed on both breasts. Further redundant skin was excised along the vertical limb incisions below the areola on both sides to accomplish symmetry. The patient was then placed back in the supine position. The wounds were closed using 4-0 chromic at the subcutaneous level followed by 5-0 nylon at the periareolar area at the skin level; this was performed in a vertical mattress continuous fashion. The vertical limbs below the areola on both breasts were both closed using 3-0 chromic at the subcutaneous level followed by 3-0 Monocryl in a running subcuticular fashion. Interrupted Monocryls were placed intermittently along both vertical limbs to relieve tension and Steri-Strips were applied. Gauze dressings and conforming bra was placed. The patient tolerated the procedure well, arrived to recovery room in stable condition.

Liberty Crouch

Any Thoughts

Enlighten Me

Several noteworthy topics for sure. Please keep in mind that I have shared my personal recorded documents from *the professionals* to you for the purpose of transparency. Please realize the significant changes in my medical history, medication management, social behaviors, mental evaluations, and even surgical procedures documented that coincide with writings from *Books 1, 2,* and *3* along with psychiatrists, psychologists, and home therapist reports of my journey, raw and unscripted all for the glory of God.

Truly the evidence of my journey shared with you can inspire you to know that nothing is impossible for God. Anything you put your faith into gives *it* power to prosper, good or evil. Generational cycles of sin can be broken through the power of God when you put your faith there. There is power in words. I spoke the things I believed. The things I spoke, I gave power to. And the things that other people, including doctors within this book, spoke over me had the power to make or break a situation.

Looking back at some of the reports, I noticed some of the exact same verbiage on notes with dates spread out for months. Even though that same verbiage was inaccurate it followed me. December 31, 2012 was an important date. It was the day I visited the psychiatrist and he denied me the very addictive drug Klonopin. This was the same day I heard the voice of God for the first time later that evening. You can read about it in *Book 2 - Truth Through Testimony - #1*.

January 28, 2013 was the day I met Jesus Christ as my personal Lord and Savior. You can read about it in *Book 2 – Truth Through Testimony #2*.

February 20, 2013 was the day of my Great Deliverance which you can read about as well in *Book 2 – Truth Through Testimony #3* and the C.I.T. (Creative Inspirational Thinking free verse poem) titled *Spiritual Warfare*.

The battle of the mind is real. That's why the Lord gave us instructions on how to be victorious within the Holy Scriptures. I remember during my progression in recovery, the Lord used me to be a witness of His name and power to *the professionals* on several occasions. In *Book 1,* I wrote a C.I.T. titled *Frankenstein I Am* which coincides with the surgeon's reports. My sole purpose for sharing with such extreme transparency, is so you can be free from the ways of the world.

I know the Way. From where I was, everything I overcame, to where I am at this present time of my life, it is only by the grace of God and His almighty love and power that brought me here. His name is Jesus. He is the Way.

Any Thoughts

False Positive Drug Tests Can Impact Your Life as if You Were Guilty

*Drugs that can cause false positives:

If you've taken one of these medications and had what you believe is a false positive test, work with your healthcare provider to see if you can stop taking the medication or cut back on it. Then ask for a confirmatory test or a repeat test.

1) **Dextromethorphan** is an active ingredient in Robitussin, Delsym, and other over-the-counter cough suppressants. If you've taken a medication with dextromethorphan in it, your drug screen may be positive for opiates and PCP (phencyclidine).

2) **Diltiazem** (Cardizem) is used to treat hypertension (high blood pressure) or to slow your heart rate if you have atrial fibrillation. If you're taking diltiazem, your urine drug screen may test as a false positive for LSD.

3) **Diphenhydramine** (Benadryl) is an antihistamine found in allergy medications like Benadryl and sleep aids like Tylenol PM and Advil PM. If you've taken diphenhydramine, your drug screen may show a positive result for opiates, methadone, or PCP.

4) **Metformin** (Glucophage) is the most commonly prescribed oral medication for diabetes. Taking metformin may result in a positive test for amphetamine or methamphetamine.

5) **Pseudoephedrine**, used for sinus and nasal congestion, (Sudafed) can be the cause of false positive tests for amphetamine or methamphetamine.

6) **Labetalol** (Trandate) is both an alpha- and beta-blocker drug used for blood pressure control. If you're taking labetalol, you could have a false positive test for amphetamine, methamphetamine, or LSD.

*Source: https://www.goodrx.com/blog/these-15-medications-can-cause-a-false-positive-on-drug-tests/ (retrieved 6/5/21 - 6 items from a list of 14 items are included) by Dr. Sharon Orrange.

Please search for reliable sources on the internet for yourself with the key words, *drugs that can cause false positives*.

Part III – The Lamb

Phone Art: What Do *You* See?
Blessings and Curses

See, I am setting before you today a blessing and a curse—the blessing if you obey the commands of the Lord your God that I am giving you today; the curse if you disobey the commands of the Lord your God and turn from the way that I command you today by following other gods, which you have not known.

Deuteronomy 11:26-28

- *Is it possible to pass down to my children habits I have in my own life?*
- *Is it possible for my children to pick up ways I modeled to them?*
- How about this, *is it possible for my children to inherit specific character traits through DNA even when they are not raised by one or both parents?*

> I believed, therefore I spoke,…
> Psalm 119:10

As a result of my own disobedience, regardless of the circumstances of life that brought me to a place of torment by following the ways of the world which were destruction to my soul (mind, will, and emotions), the way I expressed myself in words sounded very illiterate because of the way my mind thought. I had a stutter, and my thought patterns were chaotic…

But God, in His mercy has hidden His promise and kept it safe until the appointed time. I hold onto this promise, in times of remembering what God has already done, because this is a glimpse of *my* tangible evidence of God at work in my life.

> The reckless mind will gain knowledge, and the stammering tongue will speak clearly and fluently.
> Isaiah 32:4 (HCSB)

A Test:
I Let the Devil in My House
Journal Entry Dated: May 22, 2013

The devil came into my house yesterday. I did not know it at first though, but I'm alive today to tell it. Thank God because I gotta finish my mission. I have a sense of empowerment, freedom all over again, and my reason for being here is rekindled. Tears are flushing my face right now because I'm so proud of me. Nobody knows except God and now my readers' ears, for this very purpose - Truth. I was put to the ultimate test during my third year of sobriety from methamphetamines. The anniversary of my recovery date is coming up on July 4, 2013.

My neighbor knocked on my door yesterday. She just got released from the mental ward for attempting suicide, nearly lost her mind, paranoid and delusional. I saw *me* in her the day she went in, almost two weeks ago, that was the first time she knocked on my door for help. The devil had ahold of her, awfully familiar indeed. I felt so deeply sorry for her because the stories she uttered were crying for help but didn't actually ask for it. Maybe she couldn't get the right words out. I prayed with her and even in my heart as I hugged her before they took her away that day. The thing is, I called her at that recovery hospital every day for a week and read short Scriptures from the Bible to her for encouragement.

When she got out a couple of days later, she was in search of that very same self-misery and hell that put her there in the first place - meth. I knew it, I could see it all over her; by her words and actions, then she confessed it, the very thing I knew. She told me. She confided in me. She said she was going to get more meth and she couldn't help it. I could tell she was feeling convicted to do right but she was still choosing to do wrong. It's like she was powerless to make the decision to not do meth again.

I told her that we both had the same Judge, and I was not her judge. I knew her frame of mind because I'd been there before, plenty. She wouldn't listen to my sound advice. She left my house that morning and came back high as a kite on meth. Immediately thoughts came into my head like, *how easy it would be for me to get high just one more time* and *nobody would ever know*. But you see that was the devil creeping his way in. I let that thought go.

Her husband came home. She came back over to my house, this time very sketched out and paranoid. She brought her *meth stash* over with her, with the intentions to either flush it or hide it at my house until the next day when her husband would go to work. She feared he might find it and put her in jail or back in the recovery hospital. For some reason out of my own mouth I said, "No, don't flush it. Hide it till your husband leaves and come back and get it."

In the back of my mind, I said it honestly, for the intentions that I might do the meth myself. I told my neighbor later when she asked for it back that I had flushed it. We initially hid the bag of drugs (meth), in my house together. She went home and I could hear her and her husband yelling back and forth throughout the day. The walls were thin.

Her husband ended up leaving the house for a little while. She came over again and asked me for her stash. I lied and said I flushed it because I got paranoid. She thanked me for flushing her drugs and she said, "I don't want to do it anymore." She was still sketched out - hallucinating. She asked me to come to her house with her.

Her house was a mess, just torn to pieces, trash everywhere, furniture torn apart, small broken pieces of white candle wax collectively placed in specific areas, and the smell was atrocious! She kept telling me about the shadow people that were in her house.

Even though this whole situation brought me back to where I was years ago, a dark place, a place I swore off, the thoughts were still coming at me in my mind of how I could get away with doing *it* just one more time.

At this point, I had relocated the *meth stash* we initially hid together. In my thoughts, I was really trying to figure out when and where and how I could do the drugs and get away with it. My thoughts became obsessively concentrated on nothing else.

Now, some of you may not understand and may be asking the question, "Why?" and "Why did you even allow this to come into your house?"

I can honestly say, the devil works through trickery and deception. He steps in and dilutes your thought process for a short time, but long enough to convince you to listen to him. The devil and workers of iniquity try any way possible by using your emotions against you and by sending arrows of temptations and schemes into your mind, in attempts to defeat God's plan for your life. It seems the closer I get to God, the closer the devil creeps.

I straight up saw with my own eyes the half gram of meth, even held it in my hand. It was in my house for almost 24 hours. I was tempted beyond measure the whole time. Please understand that the power of God and my purpose here is greater than any simple pleasure the devil's playground has to offer but I didn't even know I was being played this day.

I know now that I am stronger than I ever knew. I prayed before I went to bed that night, "God Please Get The Devil Out Of My House!" All night I couldn't sleep. I laid in bed being tormented because I knew the devil was literally in my closet in a bathrobe pocket just waiting for me to act on my thoughts of *just one more time*.

I got out of bed the next morning with a strategic plan from God to save my life and to be able to continue my mission. I put on two pairs of rubber gloves, got the *meth stash* out of my closet, and went into the bathroom. I prayed to God in the name of Jesus, for my mind, strength, and salvation. I opened the plastic bag the drugs were in. I could feel the crystals with my fingertips even through the gloves. I dumped the drugs straight down into the toilet water and tore up the plastic bag and flushed it and flushed it again. I washed my gloves, washed my hands, threw away the gloves, and prayed again. I cried my eyes out with mixed feelings of how hard that was and with feelings of victory and an overwhelming deep sorrow of repentance.

Not only did I live this day to tell of the strength God Almighty gave me to overcome this thing, but another reason was to tell you. The girl next door didn't really need or even want the devil in her life anymore, but she didn't know how to access the strength to overcome him. To break it down for you, I lied to the neighbor ahead of time for a good reason (not knowing it), even though the intents of my heart were not good, the end results saved both of our lives that day.

There is power in the name of Jesus to overcome, and the devil knows it.

Liberty Crouch

Any Thoughts

They Said I Wouldn't Make It
A Letter from My Oldest Son

Mamma,

From my understanding this letter is of great importance. I am honored to write a letter of this nature.

First being said, I love you and Happy Mother's Day! Second, through all the years I've had the opportunity to walk and stand with you, through the good, bad, and ugly, I've always believed in you, mamma.

So now, me, being a young man, I have seen "True folding – tenfold" (slang for how Kingdom provision and purposes work).

I honor you with the up most respect. "They Said I Wouldn't Make It," one of my most favorite gospel songs. And totally, this song speaks volumes in both of our lives.

I love you and bless you!

XOXOXO, your first born aka "Student Jock"

Liberty Crouch

Through Thick and Thin

My son, son of my womb, the son I prayed for,

Thank you for your kind words. You are very humble in your expressions. I know the "walk" you refer and the position of "standing" you express, but to the readers of my dreams, I want you to know that my son expresses his love and pain in such a short and powerful letter to me.

He not only has walked with me through the shadow of death, but he has stood by me as we conquered death together through the power of Christ Jesus' shed blood and has witnessed the favor of God and His grace through the Lord's mercy and kindness. The generational cycles of sin came for him too. Addictions far and wide and the consequences of those sins were evident in his life as well. But God.

My son, we overcame by faith, by the blood of the Lamb, and by the word of our testimony. We overcame as we stood in faith and love, putting our trust in the Lord with the hope of our salvation, not loving our own ways or our own lives, that we should shrink back into the sin that separates us from God. And as you know, to be separated from God is death. What an honor to do life with you, watch you grow into the man of God you were created to be. What a joy and fullness it brings to my spirit to know it is because you believed in me as I followed Jesus Christ, that you can see the true tenfold blessings of God in your own life. Onlookers, oh well. "They said 'we' wouldn't make it," but as they watch, we continue to pray for them to overcome as well. Follow me as I follow Jesus. I thank you for believing in me and holding fast to the anchor of hope when you had all rights to abandon ship just as I did in the past. The Lord certainly blessed you with the mercy gift. You are so quick to forgive. This a true asset to living close to God, and you my son are a champion of the faith.

I love you too son, keep going, live the legacy you want to leave, I believe in you too!

Love, Mamma

There is Power in the Name of Jesus

Instead of passively just letting thoughts go, I would like to share some Scriptures that continue to empower me. I mentioned in the page titled, *A Test: I Let the Devil in My House;* the importance of taking thoughts captive.

> For though we walk in the flesh [as mortal men], we are not carrying on our [spiritual] warfare according to the flesh *and* using the weapons of man. The weapons of our warfare are not physical [weapons of flesh and blood]. Our weapons are divinely powerful for the destruction of fortresses. *We are* destroying sophisticated arguments and every exalted *and* proud thing that sets itself up against the [true] knowledge of God, and *we are* taking every thought *and* purpose captive to the obedience of Christ.
> 2 Corinthians 10:3-5 (AMP)

"You cannot be tempted in an area that you have been truly delivered by God from." LCT

"Entertaining every thought is an open invitation for thoughts to take you captive." LCT

Have you ever let the devil into your house? Now I will speak literally to you so you can see what I am saying. If your body is the temple of the Holy Spirit in which the Living God dwells; according to Scripture, then your body is the house in which I am referring to now.

> Or do you not know that your body is a temple of the Holy Spirit within you, whom you have from God? You are not your own, for you were bought with a price. So, glorify God in your body.
> 1 Corinthians 6:19-20 (ESV)

If you are a Christian, a follower of Christ, I am reminding you that your body is the house of the Lord. With that being said, we are to be mindful of the things of God and alert to the enemy's schemes that try to come in by way of our eye gates and ear gates.

In the Old Testament Scriptures, before Christ Jesus' shed blood, the high priest would enter the holy of holies and make atonement for his sins and the sins of the people by using a blood sacrifice from an animal. He went inside with a rope tied around him because if there was any unholiness about him, he would not come out alive. The people would then have to pull him out by that rope.

Today, as a Christian, in the New Testament Jesus Christ is our High Priest. He alone has made the atonement for all of mankind by shedding His holy blood on the cross of Calvary for all our sins. Today, when a believer wants to come into the holy of holies, we enter by the blood of Jesus through faith.

> Therefore, brethren, having boldness to enter the Holiest by the blood of Jesus, by a new and living way…
> Hebrews 10:19-20

When we come to the Lord, focused on Him, humbly with our sin He is faithful to forgive us and wash us clean from all unrighteousness.

> If we confess our sins, He is faithful and just to forgive us *our* sins and to cleanse us from all unrighteousness.
> 1 John 1:9

Unless I first die to myself, my self-seeking mindset, my selfishness, my self-righteousness, my self-disillusionment, intelligence, fulfilling the lusts of the flesh, and entitlement, I cannot see God in the holy of holies. The world tries to keep us so busy. We become weak and tired and look to ourselves for all the answers; this veil has blinded some people from coming all the way into the secret place. The enemies of God get busy about using our weaknesses for their own benefit.

It is the anchor of hope that Christians have in Jesus that is the symbolic rope of the high priest that allows us into the secret place, the holy of holies. Behind the second curtain, the tabernacle was called the most holy place.

> Behind the second veil there was another tabernacle [the inner one or second section] known as the Holy of Holies,
> Hebrews 9:3 (AMP)

If you are not yet a believer, a follower of Christ Jesus, I would encourage you to continue reading this book all the way through. Freedom is right around the corner…of the veil.

The devil cannot come into the holy of holies and neither can our carnal unbelieving hearts. The enemies of God Almighty cannot stay where they do not have legal access. All satan's cohorts look for access points, entrances into your heart and mind. When we let the influences of ungodliness, worldly thinking, and things that are not pleasing to God, destructive behaviors begin to manifest in our lives.

I can only imagine how the high priest felt back in the Old Testament biblical times, when it was atonement day, and he was called to go into the holy of holies. I can imagine the intense worship he must have needed to stay in such a holy mindset. All the whispers of fear that he must have had to battle within himself. And God forbid he fell into temptation the day before.

I can compare that with today's Christian deacon who lives day by day in their own strength and loses a battle of addiction on a Friday night. He then doesn't come to church on Sunday because of guilt and shame, in fear of dying to himself for whatever reason, so that Christ Jesus could be made alive within him.

I've mentioned *dying to self* a few times so let me explain. No, I'm not talking about killing yourself. I am referring to the following Scriptures that empower us:

> ["]For through the Law I died to the Law *and* its demands on me [because salvation is provided through the death and resurrection of Christ], so that I might [from now on] live to God. I have been crucified with Christ [that is, in Him I have shared His crucifixion]; it is no longer I who live, but Christ lives in me. The *life* I now live in the body I live by faith [by adhering to, relying on, and completely trusting] in the Son of God, who loved me and gave Himself up for me. I do not ignore *or* nullify the [gracious gift of the] grace of God [His amazing, unmerited favor], for if righteousness *comes* through [observing] the Law, then Christ died needlessly. [His suffering and death would have had no purpose whatsoever.]"
>
> Galatians 2:19-21 (AMP)

There is power in the name of Jesus. There is no other name greater than His name. I have experienced many times over, the power of God's love in my own life. This power transforms the heart. This power brings resurrection life. This power is also available to anyone who will believe in Jesus Christ without wavering and follow Him.

If you are believing the Lord to save someone that you've been praying for, stay the course, keep your faith, and be encouraged by my story as an overcomer. Many people prayed for me. God hears and God cares. God sees and God answers. I will believe with you that your loved ones will have salvation through Christ Jesus, because Jesus Christ's sacrifice for eternal life was made for *all*.

> "For God so [greatly] loved *and* dearly prized the world, that He [even] gave His [One and] only begotten Son, so that whoever believes *and* trusts in Him [as Savior] shall not perish, but have eternal life.["]
>
> John 3:16 (AMP)

If you have never experienced the power of God in your life, please just ask Him. Ask, seek, and find. The Lord is a rewarder of those who diligently seek Him. Humble yourself and seek His face. God honors faith. Meet with the Lord in your secret place and He will reward you openly.

> "Ask, and it will be given to you; seek, and you will find; knock, and it will be opened to you. For everyone who asks receives, and he who seeks finds, and to him who knocks it will be opened.["]
>
> Matthew 7:7-8

> But without faith *it is* impossible to please *Him,* for he who comes to God must believe that He is, and *that* He is a rewarder of those who diligently seek Him.
>
> Hebrews 11:6

> But you, when you pray, go into your room, and when you have shut your door, pray to your Father who *is* in the secret *place;* and your Father who sees in secret will reward you openly.
>
> Matthew 6:6

Why I Pray – A Testimony
From My Youngest Son, Elijah

Why I Pray

To understand *how* you gotta understand *why*. I pray because when I was a little kid with no one to talk to and I was going through the toughest times of my life, I remembered someone told me God is always there for you to talk to.

When my mom was on drugs and tried to kill herself with me, my sister, and older brother in the next room, I remembered; God is always there for you to talk to.

When I was pretty much homeless and I had to live with various family members, I remembered, and I prayed.

When I struggled with sports and thought I would never get that full ride scholarship and I would stress my family even more because I knew we couldn't afford college, I prayed.

I prayed in times of hardship because that is where I get comfort and feel secure. Every time I prayed, things changed in my life. I would pray so hard sometimes, in the midst of tears and all by myself. I could feel God there with me. I feel powerful with God, that's why I pray.

I prayed during hard times. I prayed when prayers were answered. And I continued to pray during good times.

I prayed when I got to play on my first ever sports team. I prayed before and after each practice and game. All the kids looked at me like it was funny but then our coaches started praying too.

Liberty Crouch

I prayed when my mom was healed and now after about 12 years of being clean, I still pray for her. She is the strongest lady I know. Her story is tremendous. The reason she came out of that gutter, that terrible place she was in, is because she prayed.

When my dad finally got an apartment for me and my sister, we prayed. We were so thankful because we had been separated for a time. We didn't always stay with each other when living with family members. I'm so thankful for my Dad, so I pray.

I prayed when I got my first full ride to a division one college. I prayed because it was an answered prayer.

While I may seem normal on the outside. There is a lot going on inside me. There are still battles I'm fighting but I'm not fighting alone. Jesus is there with me every step of the way. That's why I can smile.

Praying is something that takes a little faith because you are talking to the unseen and listening to voices that you probably don't know where they are coming from. But with the faith of a mustard seed anything can be accomplished through prayer.

This is why I pray.

My son, Elijah, son of God, heir of Christ Jesus,
now team captain of a division 1 college basketball team,
senior year and career honor student,
mighty prayer warrior,
I salute you in the highest honor.
Love always,
Mamma

A Letter to My Past, Present, and Future

This is a Letter to *My Past* Before Christ

In order for me, out of a pure heart, to continue growing and leading others towards the Victory that is already won, I must address the past.

To those faces that I see even now, you know who you are. I am writing you because I feel your pain. I know I left you in pain, feeling rejected, abandoned, and hopeless. I realize that I gave you promises that I have not kept and cannot keep. The way I completely used and abused you and your kindness was utterly wrong of me. At times I made you feel like I really loved you. At times I even told you that I did.

Today, I have been moved to a new place in my heart for every one of you that I have hurt in this way. In my pain, I feel yours. I want you to be healed from all feelings of rejection and feelings of abandonment. I want you to be healed from every place that feels resentment and unforgiveness towards me. What I'm asking you is to, *please forgive me for every time that I have hurt you, not because what I did was right, but because you deserve to be free from all that pain!*

My Prayer for *My Past* is This

Oh Lord my God, how merciful and loving of a Father You are!

You continue to set me free and have done a good work in me and will continue, through Your sheer grace and mercy. Oh Lord, please reach from heaven right now and save everyone I purposely hurt and unintentionally wounded from *my past* before you saved me.

Give each one of them, who You are showing me right now, a place to meet with You in their hearts. Free them from all the pain I have ever caused them. Touch each one right now with the power of the Holy Ghost and tangible presence of Your love. Fill them up with You.

Deliver them from every root of evil and ungodly stronghold, in the name of Jesus Christ of Nazareth. Release them from the prison walls that have kept them bound and heal them now oh Lord God Almighty.

Liberty Crouch

Bless them with new life, a life of forgiveness and grace, so they can serve You well in the Kingdom of God.

In the precious name of my Lord and Savior, Jesus Christ, I pray for you, *my past*. To God be all the glory. Amen.

This is a Letter to *My Present*, as a New Creation in Christ

I forgive you, even now, with such a new and fresh perspective. I choose to forgive you and release you. This temporary pain that I have been experiencing will go away soon, because I know my Healer and my Redeemer.

I have been given mercy for you because the Lord has shown me that you don't know Him or know how to go to Him. This pain I have allowed in my life, will be used to grow me in such amazingly divine ways that will be used to forcefully advance the Kingdom of God. I can actually thank God for you now and this huge life changing lesson.

Through all the turmoil and dysfunction, my relationship with my first Love has been reunited. My first Love has filled the void and brought a great hope and refreshing to my life because I trust Him. I never really left Him.

I realize you were just a distraction and an imposter. But thanks again, because what the enemy meant to destroy me, using your wounded vessel, has really brought me all the more closer to the One who will never leave me or abandoned me, my first Love, the Lord my God.

My Prayer for *My Present*

Father in heaven, thank You for restoring my soul and sending the Holy Spirit to lead me in the path of righteousness for Your namesake. I thank You Lord for blessing me with the grace I've needed along the way.

Thank You for making a clear path for the destiny You have created and designed for me to travel through. Thank You for allowing me to feel the pain that I do, so I may be able to understand the pain of others.

Father, as much as I hurt and have been hurting, I can only imagine the pain that the one who caused it is actually feeling.

Please free *my present*, from all guilt, condemnation, resentment, ungodly thoughts, pride, and bondage that *it* is currently experiencing. Create in *it*, oh Lord a clean heart for You and a steadfast Spirit within *it*. Create a place of peace and rest for *my present's* weary soul. Stop this destructive cycle that is in the life of *my present*. These generational cycles of sin will go no further. Give *my present* eyes to see and ears to hear. Give *it* a new heart and a new contrite and humble Spirit filled with Your resurrection power to overcome in order to set captives free too! My Redeemer lives.

In the name of Christ Jesus my Lord, I pray for you, *my present* - the here and now. Amen.

This is a Letter to *My Future*, In Him for Him; Thanks to My God for Him First Loving Me...

Tears, only because I long for the Day of Dawn in You.
Pain, only for what You are grieved by.
Hope keeps me and Your faith holds me.
Wisdom You give and do not spare.
Insight into the Truth of why I care.

My true love is a mighty warrior in the Lord's army. He understands my *why*. The love of my life delights in my walk and the wonders inside. He is never ashamed and never holds back. He is as bold as a lion and as strong as the wind.

My future is in his hands. He hears me when I talk, even in tongues. He extends his hand to the poor and covers their sin. *My sweet future* is radiant with life and joy.

My future is exciting and adventurous; free from the weight of all the chains and burdens of *my past* that once held me down.

My present is becoming hopefully aware of *my future* and is not jealous by far. There is no competition or envy in *my future* because they are bound from entering in. In fact, *my present* asked that *my past* be healed from everything that wasn't allowed in the gates of heaven, and *my future* heard, answered, and replied.

Liberty Crouch

My Prayer from *My Future* to You

My future sent a prayer from its very heart, and this is what was said:

It was because *my past* helped me along, for such a time as this, *my present*. You spared not and took many arrows for me. Now is the time - the here and now. Be blessed in all you put your hands to. May you prosper and be in good health even as your soul prospers.

> Beloved, I pray that you may prosper in all things and be in health, just as your soul prospers.
>
> 3 John 1:2

You are the head and not the tail. You will lend and not borrow. You will be who God created you to be, and that is in His image - holy and blameless, forgiven and loved.

> The Lord will open to you His good treasure, the heavens, to give the rain to your land in its season, and to bless all the work of your hand. You shall lend to many nations, but you shall not borrow. And the Lord will make you the head and not the tail; you shall be above only, and not be beneath, if you heed the commandments of the Lord your God, which I command you today, and are careful to observe *them*.
>
> Deuteronomy 28:12-13

You are inspired to help others be healed and share your gifts for His glory. By walking in power and authority with all boldness of His might and counsel, you release the power of God here on earth just like it is in heaven.

> For we are His workmanship, created in Christ Jesus for good works, which God prepared beforehand that we should walk in them.
>
> Ephesians 2:10

> But we have this treasure in earthen vessels, that the excellence of the power may be of God and not of us.
>
> 2 Corinthians 4:7

> For the gifts and the calling of God *are* irrevocable.
>
> Romans 11:29

You know who you are, and your purpose is clear. Today, you are walking in freedom - *sweet future*.

Father God, bless the ones who hear and receive You. Bless them today Lord, with all of Your fullness.

I pray in the Name of Your Son, Jesus Christ, Who Saved me. Amen.

Any Thoughts

The Love Letter from Heaven's Throne Room to You:
Identity, Purpose, and Authority Revealed

In the beginning was the Word, and the Word was with God, and the Word was God. He was with God in the beginning. Through him all things were made; without him nothing was made that has been made. In him was life, and that life was the light of all mankind.

John 1:1-4 (NIV)

For he chose us in him before the creation of the world to be holy and blameless in his sight. In love he predestined us for adoption to sonship through Jesus Christ, in accordance with his pleasure and will—to the praise of his glorious grace, which he has freely given us in the One he loves. In him we have redemption through his blood, the forgiveness of sins, in accordance with the riches of God's grace that he lavished on us. With all wisdom and understanding, he made known to us the mystery of his will according to his good pleasure, which he purposed in Christ, to be put into effect when the times reach their fulfillment—to bring unity to all things in heaven and on earth under Christ.

In him we were also chosen, having been predestined according to the plan of him who works out everything in conformity with the purpose of his will, in order that we, who were the first to put our hope in Christ, might be for the praise of his glory. And you also were included in Christ when you heard the message of truth, the gospel of your salvation. When you believed, you were marked in him with a seal, the promised Holy Spirit, who is a deposit guaranteeing our inheritance until the redemption of those who are God's possession—to the praise of his glory.

Ephesians 1:4-14 (NIV)

This is what the Lord of Heaven's Armies, the God of Israel, says to all the captives he has exiled to Babylon from Jerusalem: "Build homes, and plan to stay. Plant gardens, and eat the food they produce. Marry and have children. Then find spouses for them so that you may have many grandchildren. Multiply! Do not dwindle away! And work for the peace and prosperity of the city where I sent you into exile. Pray to the Lord for it, for its welfare will determine your welfare."

This is what the Lord of Heaven's Armies, the God of Israel, says: "Do not let your prophets and fortune-tellers who are with you in the land of Babylon trick you. Do not listen to their dreams, because they are telling you lies in my name. I have not sent them," says the Lord.

This is what the Lord says: "You will be in Babylon for seventy years. But then I will come and do for you all the good things I have promised, and I will bring you home again. For I know the plans I have for you," says the Lord. "They are plans for good and not for disaster, to give you a future and a hope. In those days when you pray, I will listen. If you look for me wholeheartedly, you will find me. I will be found by you," says the Lord. "I will end your captivity and restore your fortunes. I will gather you out of the nations where I sent you and will bring you home again to your own land."

Jeremiah 29:4-14 (NLT)

The word that came to Jeremiah from the Lord, saying, "Thus speaks the Lord God of Israel, saying: 'Write in a book for yourself all the words that I have spoken to you. For behold, the days are coming,' says the Lord, 'that I will bring back from captivity My people Israel and Judah,' says the Lord. 'And I will cause them to return to the land that I gave to their fathers, and they shall possess it.'"

Jeremiah 30:1-3

"'So do not be afraid, Jacob my servant; do not be dismayed, Israel,' declares the Lord. 'I will surely save you out of a distant place, your descendants from the land of their exile. Jacob will again have peace and security, and no one will make him afraid. I am with you and will save you,' declares the Lord. 'Though I completely destroy all the nations among which I scatter you, I will not completely destroy you.['] …

Jeremiah 30:10-11 (NIV)

[']But I will restore you to health and heal your wounds,' declares the Lord, 'because you are called an outcast, Zion for whom no one cares.'

Jeremiah 30:17 (NIV)

"And when that happens"—God's Decree—"it will be plain as the sun at high noon: I'll be the God of every man, woman, and child in Israel and they shall be my very own people."

This is the way God put it:

"They found grace out in the desert, these people who survived the killing. Israel, out looking for a place to rest, met God out looking for them!" God told them, "I've never quit loving you and never will. Expect love, love, and more love! And so now I'll start over with you and build you up again, dear virgin Israel. You'll resume your singing, grabbing tambourines and joining the dance. You'll go back to your old work of planting vineyards on the Samaritan hillsides, And sit back and enjoy the fruit—oh, how you'll enjoy those harvests! The time's coming when watchmen will call out from the hilltops of Ephraim: 'On your feet! Let's go to Zion, go to meet our God!'"

Oh yes, God says so:

"Shout for joy at the top of your lungs for Jacob! Announce the good news to the number-one nation! Raise cheers! Sing praises. Say, 'God has saved his people, saved the core of Israel.'

"Watch what comes next:

"I'll bring my people back from the north country And gather them up from the ends of the earth, gather those who've gone blind And those who are lame and limping, gather pregnant women, Even the mothers whose birth pangs have started, bring them all back, a huge crowd!

"Watch them come! They'll come weeping for joy as I take their hands and lead them, Lead them to fresh flowing brooks, lead them along smooth, uncluttered paths. Yes, it's because I'm Israel's Father and Ephraim's my firstborn son!

"Hear this, nations! God's Message! Broadcast this all over the world! Tell them, 'The One who scattered Israel will gather them together again. From now on he'll keep a careful eye on them, like a shepherd with his flock.' I, God, will pay a stiff ransom price for Jacob; I'll free him from the grip of the Babylonian bully The people will climb up Zion's slopes shouting with joy, their faces beaming because of God's bounty—Grain and wine and oil, flocks of sheep, herds of cattle. Their lives will be like a well-watered garden, never again left to dry up. Young women will dance and be happy, young men and old men will join in. I'll convert their weeping into laughter, lavishing comfort, invading their grief with joy. I'll make sure that their priests get three square meals a day and that my people have more than enough.'" God's Decree.

Jeremiah 31:1-14 (MSG)

Arise, my people! Let your light shine for all the nations to see! For the glory of the Lord is streaming from you. Darkness as black as night shall cover all the peoples of the earth, but the glory of the Lord will shine from you. All nations will come to your light; mighty kings will come to see the glory of the Lord upon you.

Lift up your eyes and see! For your sons and daughters are coming home to you from distant lands. Your eyes will shine with joy, your hearts will thrill, for merchants from around the world will flow to you, bringing you the wealth of many lands.

Isaiah 60:1-5 (TLB)

The Spirit of the Lord God is upon me, because the Lord has anointed me to bring good news to the suffering and afflicted. He has sent me to comfort the brokenhearted, to announce liberty to captives, and to open the eyes of the blind. He has sent me to tell those who mourn that the time of God's favor to them has come, and the day of his wrath to their enemies. To all who mourn in Israel he will give: beauty for ashes; joy instead of mourning; praise instead of heaviness. For God has planted them like strong and graceful oaks for his own glory.

And they shall rebuild the ancient ruins, repairing cities long ago destroyed, reviving them though they have lain there many generations. Foreigners shall be your servants; they shall feed your flocks and plow your fields and tend your vineyards. You shall be called priests of the Lord, ministers of our God. You shall be fed with the treasures of the nations and shall glory in their riches. Instead of shame and dishonor, you shall have a double portion of prosperity and everlasting joy.

For I, the Lord, love justice; I hate robbery and wrong. I will faithfully reward my people for their suffering and make an everlasting covenant with them. Their descendants shall be known and honored among the nations; all shall realize that they are a people God has blessed.

Let me tell you how happy God has made me! For he has clothed me with garments of salvation and draped about me the robe of righteousness. I am like a bridegroom in his wedding suit or a bride with her jewels. The Lord will show the nations of the world his justice; all will praise him. His righteousness shall be like a budding tree, or like a garden in early spring, full of young plants springing up everywhere.

Isaiah 61:1-11 (TLB)

"Listen: I will send my messenger before me to prepare the way. And then the One you are looking for will come suddenly to his Temple—the Messenger of God's promises, to bring you great joy. Yes, he is surely coming," says the Lord Almighty. "But who can live when he appears? Who can endure his coming? For he is like a blazing fire refining precious metal, and he can bleach the dirtiest garments! Like a refiner of silver he will sit and closely watch as the dross is burned away. He will purify the Levites, the ministers of God, refining them like gold or silver, so that they will do their work for God with pure hearts. Then once more the Lord will enjoy the offerings brought to him by the people of Judah and Jerusalem, as he did before. At that time my punishments will be quick and certain; I will move swiftly against wicked men who trick the innocent, against adulterers and liars, against all those who cheat their hired hands, who oppress widows and orphans, or defraud strangers, and do not fear me," says the Lord Almighty.

Liberty Crouch

"For I am the Lord—I do not change. That is why you are not already utterly destroyed, for my mercy endures forever.

"Though you have scorned my laws from earliest time, yet you may still return to me," says the Lord Almighty. "Come and I will forgive you.["] ...

Malachi 3:1-7 (TLB)

"Dear brothers, I realize that what you did to Jesus was done in ignorance; and the same can be said of your leaders. But God was fulfilling the prophecies that the Messiah must suffer all these things. Now change your mind and attitude to God and turn to him so he can cleanse away your sins and send you wonderful times of refreshment from the presence of the Lord and send Jesus your Messiah back to you again. For he must remain in heaven until the final recovery of all things from sin, as prophesied from ancient times. Moses, for instance, said long ago, 'The Lord God will raise up a Prophet among you, who will resemble me! Listen carefully to everything he tells you. Anyone who will not listen to him shall be utterly destroyed.'

Acts 3:17-23 (TLB)

My beloved brothers and sisters, the passionate desire of my heart and constant prayer to God is for my fellow Israelites to experience salvation. For I know that although they are deeply devoted to God, they are unenlightened. And since they've ignored the righteousness God gives, wanting instead to be acceptable to God because of their own works, they've refused to submit to God's faith-righteousness. For Christ is the end of the law. And because of him, God has transferred his perfect righteousness to all who believe.

Romans 10:1-4 (TPT)

... "God's living message is very close to you, as close as your own heart beating in your chest and as near as the tongue in your mouth."

And what is God's "living message"? It is the revelation of faith for salvation, which is the message that we preach. For if you publicly declare with your mouth that Jesus is Lord and believe in your heart that God raised him from the dead, you will experience salvation. The heart that believes in him receives the gift of the righteousness of God—and then the mouth confesses, resulting in salvation. For the Scriptures encourage us with these words:

"Everyone who believes in him will never be disappointed."
So then faith eliminates the distinction between Jew and non-Jew, for he is the same Lord for all people. And he has enough treasures to lavish generously upon all who call on him. And it's true:

"Everyone who calls on the Lord's name will experience new life."

Romans 10:8-13 (TPT)

Dear friends, let me give you clearly the heart of the gospel that I've preached to you—the good news that you have heartily received and on which you stand. For it is through the revelation of the gospel that you are being saved, if you fasten your life firmly to the message I've taught you, unless you have believed in vain. For I have shared with you what I have received and what is of utmost importance:

> The Messiah died for our sins,
>   fulfilling the prophecies of the scriptures.
> He was buried in a tomb
>   and was raised from the dead after three days,
>   as foretold in the scriptures.
> Then he appeared to Peter the Rock
>   and to the twelve apostles.

He also appeared to more than five hundred of his followers at the same time, most of whom are still alive as I write this, though a few have passed away. Then he appeared to Jacob and to all the apostles. Last of all he appeared in front of me, like one born prematurely, ripped from the womb.

1 Corinthians 15:1-8 (TPT)

Now, I tell you this, my brothers and sisters, flesh and blood are not able to inherit God's kingdom realm, and neither will that which is decaying be able to inherit what is incorruptible.

Listen, and I will tell you a divine mystery: not all of us will die, but we will all be transformed. It will happen in an instant—in the twinkling of his eye. For when the last trumpet is sounded, the dead will come back to life. We will be indestructible and we will be transformed. For we will discard our mortal "clothes" and slip into a body that is imperishable. What is mortal now will be exchanged for immortality. And when that which is mortal puts on immortality, and what now decays is exchanged for what will never decay, then the scripture will be fulfilled that says:

> Death is swallowed up by a triumphant victory!
> So death, tell me, where is your victory?
>   Tell me death, where is your sting?

It is sin that gives death its sting and the law that gives sin its power. But we thank God for giving us the victory as conquerors through our Lord Jesus, the Anointed One. So now, beloved ones, stand firm, stable, and enduring. Live your lives with an unshakable confidence. We know that we prosper and excel in every season by serving the Lord, because we are assured that our union with the Lord makes our labor productive with fruit that endures.

1 Corinthians 15:50-58 (TPT)

Liberty Crouch

Be cheerful with joyous celebration in every season of life. Let your joy overflow! And let gentleness be seen in every relationship, for our Lord is ever near.

Don't be pulled in different directions or worried about a thing. Be saturated in prayer throughout each day, offering your faith-filled requests before God with overflowing gratitude. Tell him every detail of your life, then God's wonderful peace that transcends human understanding, will guard your heart and mind through Jesus Christ. Keep your thoughts continually fixed on all that is authentic and real, honorable and admirable, beautiful and respectful, pure and holy, merciful and kind. And fasten your thoughts on every glorious work of God, praising him always. *Put into practice the example* of all that you have heard from me or seen in my life and the God of peace will be with you in all things.

Philippians 4:4-9 (TPT)

> Sharing words of wisdom is satisfying to your inner being.
> > It encourages you to know
> > that you've changed someone else's life.
>
> Your words are so powerful
> > that they will kill or give life,
> > and the talkative person will reap the consequences.

Proverbs 18:20-21 (TPT)

And never let ugly or hateful words come from your mouth, but instead let your words become beautiful gifts that encourage others; do this by speaking words of grace to help them.

The Holy Spirit of God has sealed you in Jesus Christ until you experience your full salvation. So never grieve the Spirit of God or take for granted his holy influence in your life. Lay aside bitter words, temper tantrums, revenge, profanity, and insults. But instead be kind and affectionate toward one another. Has God graciously forgiven you? Then graciously forgive one another in the depths of Christ's love.

Ephesians 4:29-32 (TPT)

From Peter, an apostle of Jesus the Anointed One, to the chosen ones who have been scattered like "seed" into the nations living as refugees in Pontus, Galatia, Cappadocia, and throughout *the Roman provinces of* Asia and Bithynia. *You are not forgotten*, for you have been chosen and destined by Father God. The Holy Spirit has set you apart to be God's holy ones, obedient followers of Jesus Christ who have been *gloriously* sprinkled with his blood. May God's delightful grace and peace cascade over you many times over!

Celebrate with praises the God and Father of our Lord Jesus Christ, who has shown us his extravagant mercy. For his *fountain of* mercy has given us a new life—we are reborn to experience a living, energetic hope through the resurrection of Jesus Christ from the dead. We are reborn into a perfect inheritance that can never perish, never be defiled, and never diminish. It is promised and preserved forever in the heavenly realm for you!

Through our faith, the mighty power of God constantly guards us until our *full* salvation is ready to be revealed in the last time. May the thought of this cause you to jump for joy, even though lately you've had to put up with the grief of many trials. But these only reveal the sterling core of your faith, which is far more valuable than gold that perishes, for even gold is refined by fire. *Your authentic faith* will result in even more praise, glory, and honor when Jesus the Anointed One is revealed.

You love him passionately although you have not seen him, but through believing in him you are saturated with an ecstatic joy, indescribably sublime and immersed in glory. For you are reaping the harvest of your faith—the full salvation promised you—your souls' victory!

Overcoming Grace

This salvation was the focus of the prophets who prophesied of this *outpouring of* grace that was destined for you. They made a careful search and investigation of the meaning *of their God-given prophecies* as they probed into *the mysteries* of who would fulfill them and the time period when it would all take place. The Spirit of the Anointed One was in them and was pointing prophetically to the sufferings that Christ was destined to suffer and the glories that would be released afterward. God revealed to the prophets that their ministry was not for their own benefit but for yours. And now, you have heard these things from the evangelists who preached the gospel to you through *the power of* the Holy Spirit sent from heaven—the gospel *containing wonderful mysteries* that even the angels long to get a glimpse of.

A Call to Holiness

So then, prepare your *hearts and* minds for action! Stay alert and fix your hope firmly on the marvelous grace that is coming to you. For when Jesus Christ is unveiled, *a greater measure of* grace will be released to you. As God's obedient children, never again shape your lives by the desires that you followed when you didn't know better. Instead, shape your lives to become like the Holy One who called you. For Scripture says:

> "You are to be holy, because I am holy."

Since you call on him as your heavenly Father, the impartial Judge who judges according to each one's works, live each day with holy awe and reverence throughout your time on earth. For you know that your lives were ransomed once and for all from the empty and futile way of life handed down from generation to generation. It was not a ransom payment of silver and gold, which eventually perishes, but the precious blood of Christ—who like a spotless, unblemished lamb was *sacrificed for us.*

This was part of God's plan, for he was chosen and destined for this before the foundation of the earth was laid, but he has been made manifest in these last days for you. It is through him that you now believe in God, who raised him from the dead and glorified him, so that you would fasten your faith and hope in God *alone*.

Love and Purity
Now, because of your obedience to the truth, you have purified your very souls, and this empowers you to be full of love for your fellow believers. So express this sincere love toward one another passionately and with a pure heart. For through the eternal and living Word of God you have been born again. And this "seed" that he planted within you can never be destroyed but will live *and grow* inside of you forever. For:

> Human beings are *frail and temporary*, like grass,
> and the glory of man *fleeting*
> like blossoms of the field.
> The grass dries and withers and the flowers fall off,
> but the Word of the Lord endures forever!

And this is the Word that was announced to you!

1 Peter 1 (TPT)

As for us, we have all of these great witnesses who encircle us like clouds. So we must let go of every wound that has pierced us and the sin we so easily fall into. Then we will be able to run life's marathon race with passion and determination, for the path has been already marked out before us.

We look away from the natural realm and we focus our attention *and expectation* onto Jesus who birthed faith within us and who leads us forward into faith's perfection. His example is this: Because his heart was focused on the joy of knowing that you would be his, he endured the agony of the cross and conquered its humiliation, and now sits exalted at the right hand of the throne of God!

So consider carefully how Jesus faced such intense opposition from sinners who opposed their own souls, so that you won't become worn down and cave in under life's pressures. After all, you have not yet reached the point of sweating blood in your opposition to sin. And have you forgotten his encouraging words spoken to you as his children? He said,

> "My child, don't underestimate the value
> of the discipline and training of the Lord God,
> or get depressed when he has to correct you.
>
> For the Lord's training of your life
> is the evidence of his faithful love.
> And when he draws you to himself,
> it proves you are his delightful child."

Fully embrace God's correction as part of your training, for he is doing what any loving father does for his children. For who has ever heard of a child who never had to be corrected? We all should welcome God's discipline as the validation of authentic sonship. For if we have never once endured his correction it only proves we are strangers and not sons.

And isn't it true that we respect our earthly fathers even though they corrected and disciplined us? Then we should demonstrate an even greater respect for God, our spiritual Father, as we submit to his life-giving discipline. Our parents corrected us for the short time of our childhood as it seemed good to them. But God corrects us throughout our lives for our own good, giving us an invitation to share his holiness. Now all discipline seems to be painful at the time, yet later it will produce a transformation of character, bringing a harvest of righteousness and peace to those who yield to it.

So be made strong even in your weakness by lifting up your tired hands *in prayer and worship*. And strengthen your weak knees, for as you keep walking forward on God's paths all your stumbling ways will be divinely healed!

In every relationship be swift to choose peace over competition, and run swiftly toward holiness, for those who are not holy will not see the Lord. Watch over each other to make sure that no one misses the revelation of God's grace. And make sure no one lives with a root of bitterness sprouting within them which will only cause trouble and poison the hearts of many.

Hebrews 12:1-15 (TPT)

Make very sure that you never refuse to listen to God when he speaks! For the God who spoke on earth from Sinai is the same God who now speaks from heaven. Those who heard him speak his living Word on earth found nowhere to hide, so what chance is there for us to escape if we turn our backs on God and refuse to hear his warnings as he speaks from heaven?

The earth was rocked at the sound of his voice from the mountain, but now he has promised,

> "Once and for all I will not only shake the systems of the world,
> but also the unseen powers in the heavenly realm!"

Now this phrase "once and for all" clearly indicates the final removal of things that are shaking, that is, the old order, so only what is unshakable will remain. Since we are receiving *our rights to* an unshakable kingdom we should be extremely thankful and offer God the purest worship that delights his heart as we lay down our lives in absolute surrender, filled with awe. For our God is a holy, devouring fire!

Hebrews 12:25-27 (TPT)

Then I heard a triumphant voice in heaven proclaiming:

> "Now salvation and power are set in place,
> and the kingdom reign of our God
> and the ruling authority of his Anointed One
> are established.

> For the accuser of our brothers and sisters,
> Who *relentlessly* accused them
> day and night before our God,
> has now been *defeated*—cast out once and for all!

> They conquered him completely
> through the blood of the Lamb
> and the powerful word of his testimony.

> *They triumphed because* they did not love and cling
> to their own lives, even when faced with death.

Revelation 12:10-11 (TPT)

Any Thoughts

_____
_____
_____
_____
_____
_____
_____
_____
_____
_____
_____
_____
_____

Promises of God

These are some of my favorite promises from the Scriptures that I remember when I am in combat against the lies of the enemy.

Exodus 14:14 (NIV) ["]The Lord will fight for you; you need only to be still."

Numbers 23:19 (GNT) God is not like people, who lie; He is not a human who changes his mind. Whatever he promises, he does; He speaks, and it is done.

Deuteronomy 31:8 (NIV) ["]The Lord himself goes before you and will be with you; he will never leave you nor forsake you. Do not be afraid; do not be discouraged."

Joshua 1:9 (NIV) ["]Have I not commanded you? Be strong and courageous. Do not be afraid; do not be discouraged, for the Lord your God will be with you wherever you go."

2 Chronicles 7:14 (NIV) if my people, who are called by my name, will humble themselves and pray and seek my face and turn from their wicked ways, then I will hear from heaven, and I will forgive their sin and will heal their land.

Isaiah 32:4 (HCSB) The reckless mind will gain knowledge, and the stammering tongue will speak clearly and fluently.

Isaiah 41:10 (NIV) So do not fear, for I am with you; do not be dismayed, for I am your God. I will strengthen you and help you; I will uphold you with my righteous right hand.

Isaiah 41:13 (NIV) For I am the Lord your God who takes hold of your right hand and says to you, Do not fear; I will help you.

Isaiah 43:1-7 (NIV) But now, this is what the Lord says—he who created you, Jacob, he who formed you, Israel: "Do not fear, for I have redeemed you; I have summoned you by name; you are mine. When you pass through the waters, I will be with you; and when you pass through the rivers, they will not sweep over you. When you walk through the fire, you will not be burned; the flames will not set you ablaze. For I am the Lord your God, the Holy One of Israel, your Savior; I give Egypt for your ransom, Cush and Seba in your stead. Since you are precious and honored in my sight, and because I love you, I will give people in exchange for you, nations in exchange for your life. Do not be afraid, for I am with you; I will bring your children from the east and gather you from the west. I will say to the north, 'Give them up!' and to the south, 'Do not hold them back.' Bring my sons from afar and my daughters from the ends of the earth—everyone who is called by my name, whom I created for my glory, whom I formed and made."

Isaiah 49:25 (NKJV) … For I will contend with him who contends with you, And I will save your children.

Isaiah 51:16 (NKJV) And I have put My words in your mouth; I have covered you with the shadow of My hand, That I may plant the heavens, Lay the foundations of the earth, And say to Zion, 'You *are* My people.'"

Jeremiah 29:11 (NIV) ["]For I know the plans I have for you," declares the Lord, "plans to prosper you and not to harm you, plans to give you hope and a future.["]

Ezekiel 36:26 (NKJV) I will give you a new heart and put a new spirit within you; I will take the heart of stone out of your flesh and give you a heart of flesh.

Psalm 23:4 (NIV) Even though I walk through the darkest valley, I will fear no evil, for you are with me; your rod and your staff, they comfort me.

Psalm 27:1 (NIV) The Lord is my light and my salvation—whom shall I fear? The Lord is the stronghold of my life—of whom shall I be afraid?

Psalm 32:8 (KJV) I will instruct thee and teach thee in the way which thou shalt go: I will guide thee with mine eye.

Psalm 34:17 (NIV) The righteous cry out, and the Lord hears them; he delivers them from all their troubles.

Psalm 37:4 (NIV) Take delight in the Lord, and he will give you the desires of your heart.

Psalm 37:23-24 (NIV) The Lord makes firm the steps of the one who delights in him; though he may stumble, he will not fall, for the Lord upholds him with his hand.

Proverbs 3:5-6 (NIV) Trust in the Lord with all your heart and lean not on your own understanding; in all your ways submit to him, and he will make your paths straight.

Proverbs 22:6 (NIV) Start children off on the way they should go, and even when they are old they will not turn from it.

Matthew 6:31-34 (NLT) "So don't worry about these things, saying, 'What will we eat? What will we drink? What will we wear?' These things dominate the thoughts of unbelievers, but your heavenly Father already knows all your needs. Seek the Kingdom of God above all else, and live righteously, and he will give you everything you need. So don't worry about tomorrow, for tomorrow will bring its own worries. Today's trouble is enough for today.["]

Matthew 11:28-29 (NIV) "Come to me, all you who are weary and burdened, and I will give you rest. Take my yoke upon you and learn from me, for I am gentle and humble in heart, and you will find rest for your souls.["]

Mark 11:24 (NIV) Therefore I tell you, whatever you ask for in prayer, believe that you have received it, and it will be yours.

Luke 11:9-13 (NIV) "So I say to you: Ask and it will be given to you; seek and you will find; knock and the door will be opened to you. For everyone who asks receives; the one who seeks finds; and to the one who knocks, the door will be opened. "Which of you fathers, if your son asks for a fish, will give him a snake instead? Or if he asks for an egg, will give him a scorpion? If you then, though you are evil, know how to give good gifts to your children, how much more will your Father in heaven give the Holy Spirit to those who ask him!"

John 3:16 (NIV) For God so loved the world that he gave his one and only Son, that whoever believes in him shall not perish but have eternal life.

John 3:36 (NIV) Whoever believes in the Son has eternal life, but whoever rejects the Son will not see life, for God's wrath remains on them.

John 8:36 (NIV) So if the Son sets you free, you will be free indeed.

John 11:25-26 (NIV) Jesus said to her, "I am the resurrection and the life. The one who believes in me will live, even though they die; and whoever lives by believing in me will never die.["]...

John 13:34-35 (VOICE) So I give you a new command: Love each other *deeply and fully*. Remember the ways that I have loved you, and demonstrate your love for others in those same ways. Everyone will know you as My followers if you demonstrate your love to others.

John 14:1-4 (TPT) "Don't worry or surrender to your fear. For you've believed in God, now trust and believe in me also. My Father's house has many dwelling places. If it were otherwise, I would tell you plainly, because I go to prepare a place for you. And when everything is ready, I will come back and take you to myself so that you will be where I am. And you already know the way to the place where I'm going."

John 14:15-21 (TPT) "Loving me empowers you to obey my commands. And I will ask the Father and he will give you another Savior, the Holy Spirit of Truth, who will be to you a friend just like me—and he will never leave you. The world won't receive him because they can't see him or know him. But you know him intimately because he remains with you and will live inside you."I promise that I will never leave you helpless or abandon you as orphans—I will come back to you! Soon I will leave this world and they will see me no longer, but you will see me, because I will live again, and you will come alive too. So when that day comes, you will know that I am living in the Father and that you are one with me, for I will be living in you. Those who truly love me are those who obey my commands. Whoever passionately loves me will be passionately loved by my Father. And I will passionately love him in return and will reveal myself to him."

John 14:27-31 (TPT) "I leave the gift of peace with you—my peace. Not the kind of fragile peace given by the world, but my perfect peace. Don't yield to fear or be troubled in your hearts—instead, be courageous! "Remember what I've told you, that I must go away, but I promise to come back to you. So if you truly love me, you will be glad for me, since I'm returning to my Father, who is greater than I. So when all of these things happen, you will still trust and cling to me. I won't speak with you much longer, for the ruler of this dark world is coming. But he has no power over me, *for he has nothing to use against me.* I am doing exactly what the Father destined for me to accomplish, so that the world will discover how much I love my Father. Now come with me."

John 16:33 (NIV) "I have told you these things, so that in me you may have peace. In this world you will have trouble. But take heart! I have overcome the world."

Acts 3:16 (TLB) "Jesus' name has healed this man—and you know how lame he was before. Faith in Jesus' name—faith given us from God—has caused this perfect healing.["]

Acts 26:22-23 (NIV) ["]But God has helped me to this very day; so I stand here and testify to small and great alike. I am saying nothing beyond what the prophets and Moses said would happen—that the Messiah would suffer and, as the first to rise from the dead, would bring the message of light to his own people and to the Gentiles."

Romans 5:8 (NIV) But God demonstrates his own love for us in this: While we were still sinners, Christ died for us.

Romans 8:28 (NIV) And we know that in all things God works for the good of those who love him, who have been called according to his purpose.

Romans 8:31-35 (NIV) What, then, shall we say in response to these things? If God is for us, who can be against us? He who did not spare his own Son, but gave him up for us all—how will he not also, along with him, graciously give us all things? Who will bring any charge against those whom God has chosen? It is God who justifies. Who then is the one who condemns? No one. Christ Jesus who died—more than that, who was raised to life—is at the right hand of God and is also interceding for us. Who shall separate us from the love of Christ? Shall trouble or hardship or persecution or famine or nakedness or danger or sword?

1 Corinthians 10:13 (NKJV) No temptation has overtaken you except such as is common to man; but God *is* faithful, who will not allow you to be tempted beyond what you are able, but with the temptation will also make the way of escape, that you may be able to bear *it*.

2 Corinthians 10:3-6 (NKJV) For though we walk in the flesh, we do not war according to the flesh. For the weapons of our warfare *are* not carnal but mighty in God for pulling down strongholds, casting down arguments and every high thing that exalts itself against the knowledge of God, bringing every thought into captivity to the obedience of Christ, and being ready to punish all disobedience when your obedience is fulfilled.

Ephesians 2:4-10 (NIV) But because of his great love for us, God, who is rich in mercy, made us alive with Christ even when we were dead in transgressions—it is by grace you have been saved. And God raised us up with Christ and seated us with him in the heavenly realms in Christ Jesus, in order that in the coming ages he might show the incomparable riches of his grace, expressed in his kindness to us in Christ Jesus. For it is by grace you have been saved, through faith—and this is not from yourselves, it is the gift of God—not by works, so that no one can boast. For we are God's handiwork, created in Christ Jesus to do good works, which God prepared in advance for us to do.

Ephesians 3:16-19 (NIV) I pray that out of his glorious riches he may strengthen you with power through his Spirit in your inner being, so that Christ may dwell in your hearts through faith. And I pray that you, being rooted and established in love, may have power, together with all the Lord's holy people, to grasp how wide and long and high and deep is the love of Christ, and to know this love that surpasses knowledge—that you may be filled to the measure of all the fullness of God.

Philippians 4:6-9 (NIV) Do not be anxious about anything, but in every situation, by prayer and petition, with thanksgiving, present your requests to God. And the peace of God, which transcends all understanding, will guard your hearts and your minds in Christ Jesus. Finally, brothers and sisters, whatever is true, whatever is noble, whatever is right, whatever is pure, whatever is lovely, whatever is admirable—if anything is excellent or praiseworthy—think about such things. Whatever you have learned or received or heard from me, or seen in me—put it into practice. And the God of peace will be with you.

1 Thessalonians 4:14 (NIV) For we believe that Jesus died and rose again, and so we believe that God will bring with Jesus those who have fallen asleep in him.

2 Timothy 1:7 (NLT) For God has not given us a spirit of fear and timidity, but of power, love, and self-discipline.

Liberty Crouch

James 1:5 (NIV) If any of you lacks wisdom, you should ask God, who gives generously to all without finding fault, and it will be given to you.

James 4:7 (NIV) Submit yourselves, then, to God. Resist the devil, and he will flee from you.

1 Peter 1:3 (NIV) Praise be to the God and Father of our Lord Jesus Christ! In his great mercy he has given us new birth into a living hope through the resurrection of Jesus Christ from the dead,

1 Peter 2:24 (NIV) "He himself bore our sins" in his body on the cross, so that we might die to sins and live for righteousness; "by his wounds you have been healed."

Revelation 3:5 (NIV) The one who is victorious will, like them, be dressed in white. I will never blot out the name of that person from the book of life, but will acknowledge that name before my Father and his angels.

Revelation 20:6 (NIV) Blessed and holy are those who share in the first resurrection. The second death has no power over them, but they will be priests of God and of Christ and will reign with him for a thousand years.

Search the Scriptures for your anchor in times of combat. Remember the war is for your soul and the battle is in your mind. But God who is rich in mercy gives us the victory in Christ Jesus. So, stand and declare victory over your mind, will, and emotions.

Ephesians 6:10-20 (NIV) Finally, be strong in the Lord and in his mighty power. Put on the full armor of God, so that you can take your stand against the devil's schemes. For our struggle is not against flesh and blood, but against the rulers, against the authorities, against the powers of this dark world and against the spiritual forces of evil in the heavenly realms. Therefore put on the full armor of God, so that when the day of evil comes, you may be able to stand your ground, and after you have done everything, to stand. Stand firm then, with the belt of truth buckled around your waist, with the breastplate of righteousness in place, and with your feet fitted with the readiness that comes from the gospel of peace. In addition to all this, take up the shield of faith, with which you can extinguish all the flaming arrows of the evil one. Take the helmet of salvation and the sword of the Spirit, which is the word of God. And pray in the Spirit on all occasions with all kinds of prayers and requests. With this in mind, be alert and always keep on praying for all the Lord's people. Pray also for me, that whenever I speak, words may be given me so that I will fearlessly make known the mystery of the gospel, for which I am an ambassador in chains. Pray that I may declare it fearlessly, as I should.

Write

Write down all these things I am going to do, says the Lord, and seal them up for the future. Entrust them to some godly man to pass on down to godly men of future generations.

Isaiah 8:16 (TLB)

Liberty Crouch

Liberty Crouch

Liberty Crouch

Liberty Crouch

What's to Come

Many lives were affected along my journey, some good and some bad. Hearing the back stories from my children of how my destructive behaviors and moral choices affected each one of them personally, mentally, and how it set their destiny on course, are a driving force for me to share my story to help others.

Journal entries of testimonies, footsteps of my path that brought me to where I am, divine moments in time, holy angels on assignment to ensure my mission is completed, and unexpected twists and turns that I like to say are not coincidences, will be coming to you with an array of digital fine artwork to express the visions in the most vivid way in my next book titled, *Unchained.*

Stay Connected

www.ingramcontent.com/pod-product-compliance
Lightning Source LLC
Chambersburg PA
CBHW071430070526
44578CB00001B/62